TEMPEST
in the
CLOUD

The Pathway to Spirit

A Biblical Interpretation

Aaron Anderson

And as Moses lifted up the serpent in the wilderness,

even must the Son of Man be lifted up.

–John 3:14

CONTENTS

FOREWORD 1

INTRODUCTION 13

GENESIS: *An Introduction to the Body's Energy Centers* 21

EXODUS: *The Journey Out of Lower Consciousness* 39

FOOTNOTES 111

eBook: 978-0-692-04147-5
Copyright: Aaron Anderson, 2023. All rights reserved.

FOREWORD

As you begin reading this book, take a moment to think about your life. Perhaps you're sitting by a window or reading outside under a sun-filled sky. You may be at home, or at school, or perhaps even on vacation. You might be taking a break from household chores, gardening, or any number of daily tasks that need your attention. Chances are you're settled into the routine of your life. Take this time now to move beyond your everyday habits, give yourself a minute of undistracted presence so that you can take an intimate look at your life. Are you happy, content, and peaceful?

Now go a bit deeper into your inner life. Does your mind come to a restful state easily? What types of issues tend to rise to the surface for you? Are you thriving in your relationships? With your mate, parents, children, friends, coworkers, and neighbors? Are you satisfied with your status in life? How about your career? Or with the rules of the society you live in? Will anyone be there to take care of you when you're old? For the purposes of this book, we'll call this awareness you have about yourself and the world around you *consciousness*.

Consciousness ebbs and flows with time. Everyone experiences different states of consciousness. People are at different places in their lives and so experience different levels of awareness. Consciousness fluctuates throughout time, throughout the day, weeks, and years depending on your level of presence in any given situation.

Now move your awareness even deeper into your inner life. Do you have any issues that simmer somewhere just below the surface of everyday life? Issues you can't seem to stop thinking about. Do you experience jealousy, anger, fear, or low-self esteem? Perhaps something has happened in your life that caused you to experience anxiety, distress, sadness, or discomfort. How do you react when someone cuts you off in traffic or dismisses your point of view in a conversation? Have you received poor customer service at a bank, restaurant, or store? Have you lost a loved one to violence? Do you experience lust, desire, and longing for something you will never attain? Are you sure you'll always be able to afford your home, medical bills, and food? How do you feel watching the news? If you're like most people, when you think deeply about your life you may experience some sense of unease. This unease is also part of our consciousness. Since this level of consciousness is associated with a sense of unease we will call it *lower consciousness*.

Now, think about some of the more uplifting times in your life. Think about a beautiful sunset, a hike on a sunny day, a chance sighting of a dolphin at the beach, or the view atop a scenic mountain. Think about the inspiration you get from a motivational speaker, the joy you experience from helping someone in need, or the time a stranger made your day with an act of kindness. Think about the feeling you get when you have an intellectual breakthrough and a difficult idea or concept becomes clear to you. Think about the connection you have with a cherished pet, child, or friend. These encounters are also consciousness. Since these experiences are generally associated with a feeling of well-being we will call this level of awareness *higher consciousness.*

Throughout our lives we oscillate between different levels of consciousness—between lower and higher states of being. Since most people would prefer to live in a state of peace (over a state of unease) people have sought out ways in which to remain in higher states of consciousness since perhaps the beginning of mankind.

Now, let's move beyond our personal experiences. Think about your family, friends, and the people in your community, state, and the world as a whole. Think about our shared human experiences. Are we as a people on the right path? Are you concerned about world events? In 2018 there's hardly any place on earth not experiencing massive, transformational changes. Whether it's in the area of climate, politics, economics, science, technology, gender equality, or religion—the world is rapidly transforming. The ever-changing experience we humans are sharing together is called *collective consciousness.*

Where do you find solace in an unsteady world? Where do you go for answers to your deepest questions about life? Can your mate, or parent, teacher, doctor, pastor, or president provide you with the information you need to find peace of mind? Do you believe in a higher power?

Let's confront the metaphorical elephant in the book; *Tempest in the Cloud* is about religion. We will have a serious discussion about the state of religion, specifically Christianity, and its ability to address core human issues. Are you religious (or perhaps you prefer the term spiritual)? Is Christianity serving you? Or does religion leave you with more questions than answers? Religions were created to help answer the persistent questions humans have had since the beginning of time; questions about our personal and shared consciousness. Who are we? Why are we here? And what will happen to us at death?

The purpose of this book is threefold:

1) To illustrate that God exists and can be personally, directly knowable.

2) To uncover the hidden secrets within the Bible, secret and sacred wisdom that teaches the pathway to the knowable God which happens through deep meditation practices.

3) To show the universality of the pathway to God among the world's true religions.

If you believe recent news headlines, Christianity, is on a downward slide in terms of popularity. There seems to be a lack of connection for many people between the teachings of spiritual leaders like Jesus, and the teachings of organized, institutionalized religion. Is there a problem with the written works of Christianity, or is there a problem with how the written works are interpreted by humans? *Tempest in the Cloud* makes the argument that the fault is not in the teachings of Jesus—which focuses on love, compassion, generosity, and God, but in the way that the institutionalized church has misunderstood the Bible and passed onto its congregations an incomplete understanding of the profoundness inherent in the biblical stories.

In the West, few would argue about the defining role Christianity has had in the development of the Western world. How the Bible is taught is relevant to everyone. There are still large segments of society that base their opinions, and their votes, on how they interpret the Bible. Slavery, female equality, gay rights, human sexuality, and immigration are just some of the issues that have been maligned by the misuse and misunderstanding of Jesus' teaching. Churches across the United States (and the world) have used the Bible to control and subjugate minority populations for hundreds of years. This radical misunderstanding of biblical lessons affects the entire society, not just those who practice Christianity.

Understanding the truth of Jesus' teachings is imperative to our civilization—particularly at this time of rapid transformation. The invaluable lessons of the Bible show the reader the path out of lower consciousness; the path out of the illusory identification with the physical components of life. The Bible's emphasis is on the path to spiritual consciousness that leads to Self-realization of man's true identity as a soul that is at one with God. This "straightway path" (as the Bible calls it) is a path designed by God to bring humans out of the sorrows of life that are inherent in mankind's addiction to materiality. This pathway is inside our human bodies. This pathway leads to higher states of consciousness known to religions around the world as Buddha, Krishna, or Christ Consciousness. This exalted state of consciousness is the "omniscient (all-knowing) Intelligence of God."[1] This inner body pathway is an energetic phenomenon that religions across the globe have written extensively about for thousands of years. In certain schools of the Hindu religion, this mechanism for raising consciousness is the Sanskrit word *Kundalini.*

Kundalini is a power that lies mostly dormant in every human—regardless of religious affiliation, regardless if you are agnostic, and regardless if you are an atheist. Kundalini is the vehicle for the highest states of consciousness available to humans. Right about now you may be thinking to yourself, "I go to church and I've never heard of Kundalini before!" If you have never heard of Kundalini, or the pathway to spiritual consciousness that lies inside of you, that is a failure of organized religion.

The mystics of Judaism and Christianity, along with others

who have lived the Kundalini experience, know that Kundalini is the secret teaching of the Bible. Kundalini is the driver for ascending everyday consciousness (this is also referred to as ascension or resurrection) that turned Jesus the man into Jesus the Enlightened Christ. The Bible, when understood as instructions on raising consciousness to the spirit level, is profoundly relevant to every living person. The Bible as it is taught today (mostly literally) is not that relevant to most people. To find out how organized Christianity got off track, and to understand how biblical scriptures have been misunderstood by the masses, we need to understand some basic information about how Christianity became a major global religion.

Christianity came about under the Roman Empire at a time when it was illegal to worship anything other than traditional Roman deities. Early followers of Jesus were often subjected to imprisonment or death for practicing their faith, so the early worshippers of Jesus kept a low profile to avoid persecution. Two distinct types of Christian groups were developing in the Roman Empire at that time: one being the *church* and the other being the *monastic movement*. The monastic movement consisted of thousands of monks living individually in desert isolation or in groups in communal villages. Unlike the loosely organized monasteries, the church created a strict hierarchy of bishops, priests, and deacons within territorial dioceses. This organizational "rank" structure was similar to that of the Roman government. These two groups, the church and the monasteries, were independent of each other and had different methods of practicing Jesus'

teachings. An important distinguishing difference between the church and the monasteries is the fact that the monks had a tradition of dedicated, disciplined meditation practice and the church did not.

Christianity became a prominent religion when the imperial ruler, Constantine, adopted Christ as his patron the day before he won a decisive battle for control within the empire. As a new ruler of Rome, Constantine gave unprecedented political power, along with access to the empire's financial holdings[2], to the most organized group of Christians: the church known as Catholic (a term meaning 'universal').

To understand the significance of this divide between the meditating monks and the non-meditating church we need to take a step further back into history to the time of Jesus and the apostles. When Jesus became enlightened (i.e. became Christ Consciousness) he shared his knowledge with his twelve apostles. The apostles began to write down Jesus' teaching into two types of books; "some writing 'open' books and others 'secret' books."[3] The open books were to be shared with the masses, and the secret books were to be shared only with the "spiritually stable."[4]

The meditating monks read both the open and secret books. They were uniquely qualified to understand the hidden messages within Jesus' teaching since it is meditation that creates the conditions for the ascension (enlightenment) process. The non-meditating bishops—like Dionysius (who said about the New Testament's closing book The Revelation of Saint John the Divine "I do not understand it, but I suspect that some deeper meaning is hidden in the words"[5]) apparently didn't understand the secret teaching embedded within the writing of important scriptures.

As popularity of Christianity grew throughout the Roman

Empire, competition for new converts grew between the monasteries and the Catholic Church. With the help of Emperor Constantine, the church wrestled control of the monasteries away from the independent monks (often times through intimidation, deceit, and violence[6]) under the guidance of Dionysius' successor—the influential Bishop Athanasius[7].

The secret books were starkly different than the Catholic Church's official teaching. For instance, In The Secret Revelation of John, Jesus reveals to John that God is infinite light, or *primordial consciousness*[8]. John asks Jesus if "God's Spirit comes to everyone, or only to certain people? Jesus answers that salvation is available to *everyone,* since God's Spirit is essential for life: The power enters into every man, for without (the spirit) they could not even stand upright.'[9],[10] This goes directly against the Catholic Church's assertion that only Christians can make it into heaven.

Another example of the divide between the Catholic Church and Jesus' message comes from The Secret Revelation of James. In it Jesus tells his brother James, and his disciple Peter, that God can only be known experientially through an inner "gnosis"[11] (knowledge of spiritual mysteries). These secret writings "tend to prescribe arduous prayer (meditation), study, and spiritual discipline"[12] similar to esoteric Buddhism, Hinduism, and Kabbalistic (mystic Judaism) methods. In The Secret Revelation of James, Jesus encourages his followers to "become better than I; make yourselves like the son of the Holy Spirit!"[13] The secret books encourage a personal union with God. The Gospel of Philip urges people to become "no longer a Christian, but a Christ."[14] The Bible, as we will see in the second chapter of *Tempest in the Cloud,* contains specific instructions on how a person can literally become their own Christ Consciousness with the help of Kundalini and divine guidance.

In another of the secret books, The Gospel of Truth, the "resurrection" of the physical body is described as being not literal, but instead "a shift in consciousness."[15] It is a "transformation," and a "transition into newness."[16] This shift in consciousness is also known as the "second birth" or being "born again."

The secret writings direct people to devote themselves personally to spiritual practice and to seek direct contact with God. Thus the need for clergy is bypassed. The bishops tended to suppress these writings since the need for the church was nullified. The Bishop Irenaeus once said "outside the church there is no salvation." The church's view ran contrary to the teaching of the secret books. Bishop Athanasius declared original human thinking to be "evil,"[17] and ordered Christians to reject the banned books. The secret books were deemed heretical by a bishop who obviously never meditated, and apparently did not understand how the ascension process of raising consciousness to the spiritual level occurs within the human body. Athanasius' approved "open" books went on to comprise the current canon of the New Testament, which significantly doesn't happen until nearly 400 years *after* the beginnings of early Christianity.

Unlike the censoring bishops, the monks saw the secret books as "trustworthy guides for those willing to leap into the unknown."[18] When Athanasius ordered the secret books to be destroyed, unknown persons buried copies of the secret books near monastic grounds in an area called Nag Hammadi, Egypt. The cache of books and other sacred writings were discovered 1,600 years later (in 1945) and have become known as the "Gnostic Bible" (gnostic is defined as 'relating to knowledge, especially esoteric mystical knowledge').

It has been over two thousand years since Jesus lived in the Roman Empire. Are we as a people now "spiritually stable" enough to understand the secret of becoming our own Christ Consciousness? Are we ready to understand the power of God that is already in our physical bodies? Are we ready to take the path to higher consciousness away from the mental and emotional toil that is lower consciousness? Are we ready to discover within both the open and secret sacred texts the profound teachings of Jesus that move beyond simplistic parables?

If you think the Bible is simply Jewish mythology, or a book just about the political and religious life of ancient people, you will need to intellectually move beyond those confining points of view to be open to the profound, and confounding, reality of our own energetic make-up. The Bible is a tapestry woven with three threads: literal, contextual, and esoteric. Organized religion tends to focus on the literal rendition of the biblical stories. Intellectuals and academia seem to focus on the historical/political/cultural context of the stories. *Tempest in the Cloud* focuses on the esoteric aspects of the Bible since it is the hidden knowledge of the scriptures that leads to the radical transformation of the soul. The Bible is a guide to the human body, as it is the human body that is the mechanism for resurrection. Resurrection (the second birth or ascension) that was available to Jesus *and* available to us all. The Bible does not belong to a specific church. It is not the sole property of Catholics or any other group. The Bible is a book for everyone. The Bible is a guide for *you*. The Bible teaches us how to raise our consciousness so that we can have a direct and knowable connection with God.

Tempest in the Cloud is meant to be an introduction to the spiritual awakening process. The author has firsthand knowledge of Kundalini and the ascension process. Both of which are primary topics covered in this book. The book was written under the direction of divine guidance and to the best of the author's abilities. The contents of this book are not guesses, but informed interpretations realized from research and an intuitive knowing that comes from lived experience. The author personally utilized the techniques written about in the Bible to raise their own consciousness to the Spirit level. And although the author has lived and authenticated the spiritual teaching within this book, the author is not attempting to be a spiritual teacher. The book is meant to be a personal testimonial so that other laypeople can better understand the purposes, ways, and methods of meditation and the connection it can bring forward with divinity. The author has done their best to interpret the Bible as accurately as possible. Where practical the author cross-references certain concepts with other significant religions to show the universality of the pathway to God. Hinduism in particular, widely considered the oldest of the world's religions, is referenced throughout the book to illustrate the primary connectivity of the human religious experience.

In writing this book, the author found several sources to be particularly insightful. Elaine Pagels' collection of written work on the history of Christianity moves far beyond the hyperbole of the institutional Church. Her writing brings about a new appreciation of the factual Jesus and his teaching. Pagels' in-depth academic research offers novel insights on precisely how Jesus' teachings became misinterpreted by the masses. A second important source was Paramahansa Yogananda, who is widely recognized as one of the preeminent spiritual figures in modern times. His seminal work entitled *The Second Coming of Christ: The Resurrection of the Christ Within You* is referenced in several places in this book. Yogananda's book consists of two large volumes with a wealth of inspired insight that can only be explained by someone who has dedicated their life to knowing and teaching the enlightened wisdom of both the Hindu Krishna and the Christian Christ. A third source the author engaged to make connections between the meditation instructions embedded in the Bible and those found in Hindu scriptures is Swami Satyananda Saraswati's book entitled *Kundalini Tantra*. The complex breathing techniques mentioned in the Bible are explained and illustrated in Saraswati's formative written work.

As you read any work about the spiritual journey, it is beneficial to keep in mind Yogananda's observation on the varying, often times contradicting, religious scriptures "God must enjoy the heterogeneous medley in His human family, for He has not troubled Himself to write clear directions across the heavens for all alike to see and follow in unity."[19] The basics of all true religions are the same. The path to divinity is universal, but the details inherent to the varying scriptures are heavily inspired by one's particular culture and historical time period. Sanskrit scriptures say: 'There are many sages with their scriptural and spiritual interpretations, apparently contradictory, but the real secret of religion is hidden in a cave."[20] "True religion lies within oneself, in the cave of stillness, the cave of calm intuitive wisdom, in the cave of the spiritual eye (third eye)."[21]

To know God, and to get the guidance of the Holy Spirit, one must experience the spiritual journey personally; you must discover and understand your own inner life through deep contemplation, meditation, prayer, and effort. *Tempest in the Cloud* is a guidebook to help you understand the profound inner journey that must be taken to realize the highest state of consciousness available to humans.

INTRODUCTION

As the Bible states at the beginning of Genesis, we are made in God's image. It just may not be the image many of us have in mind. Michelangelo's famous mural on the ceiling of the Vatican's Sistine Chapel illustrates God as an old man reaching out to Adam. In Western culture, God is male. We reference God as "him." But what if God is not a human form and actually has both male and female creative agencies? What if God is energy? Wouldn't we also be energy? Are we eternal energy that has temporarily incarnated on Earth in a human form? A physical body animated by immaterial, conscious energy?

If we are energy, how does that energy connect with our material form? There must be connection points within our body where the physical and subtle meet. The Hindu religion has identified areas along the spinal cord where this energy is said to enter into the body. The Sanskrit term for these areas are called *chakras*—energy centers of the human body. Does the Bible recognize these energy centers? The answer is a resounding "Yes!" The point of *Tempest in the Cloud* is to show how the writers of the Bible imbedded the scriptures with the sacred knowledge of the body's energy centers into its stories, thereby continuing the world's written history of the energetic reality of the human condition. These energy centers regulate *everything* about who we are as humans. The combined energy creates the totality of who we are emotionally, mentally, sexually, and spiritually and is collectively called *consciousness.*

Why would the writers of the Bible mask the truth about the reality of God and our own energetic selves? Throughout the history of man, the writers of sacred scriptures have used metaphors to hide universal truths about our place in the universe. Made necessary by an intellectually unprepared populous and tyranical religious and political powers. Jail or death was the usual punishment for anyone willing to speak openly about the true nature of mankind, particularly if it threatened the controlling ways of the ruling elite. So the mystics of every culture—the people who sought, and learned, the meaning of life—used a device known as anthropomorphism to document their discoveries about the human condition. Anthropomorphism is defined as **ascribing human form or attributes to a being or thing not human, particularly a deity**. To sooth a population that wasn't yet mentally prepared for the reality of the human condition, religions personified God, and the variety of energies that make up consciousness, into human-formed gods and goddesses. These anthropomorphic rendered characters, like Michelangelo's male-figured God, helped to convey complex ideas about our relationship with the divine into simplified, easily understood parables. The formless energy that creates life was made into human form—a form that people of antiquity could relate upon. Humanity may now be evolving beyond these metaphorical explanations of human life to the point we can unpack the meaning of scriptural stories to begin to understand our true energetic make up.

Every living being has consciousness. Consciousness is an accumulation of life-enabling vital energies that animate our human form. Our physical body would be inert without this divine power. This conscious energy flows through every human being regardless of one's religion. This energy is what makes us human. Without this energy our bodies would not have life. The physical aspect of our being is temporary. It decays. Our energetic selves are eternal and not dependent on a physical form.

To better understand the differences between the multiple energies that make up human consciousness, religious traditions, including Christianity, have divided consciousness into three main categories: Animal, Human, and Spiritual. All humans have a varying degree of all three of these types of energy. This is why most stories in the Bible contain the three elements—animals, humans, and the *potential* of spiritual enlightenment—within any particular story. Reaching the 'Spiritual' level is the goal of human life.

Our lowest level of consciousness is called 'Animal' because it is our densest state of being. This is a state we share with animals that rule our most basic instincts such as survival, security, pack mentality, carnal desires, and reproductive impulses. The next level of refinement, the 'Human' part of our consciousness represents a higher level of being that distinguishes humans from animals. This level of being rules our ability for higher-order communication skills and creative expression. The 'Spiritual' part of consciousness is the highest state of being available to humans and regulates the more refined aspects of living such as intuition, transcendence, wisdom, and self-awareness.

These three aspects of consciousness—Animal, Human, and Spiritual, are contained within the human body as energy. This energy enters our bodies at energy centers that are dispersed along our spines near the major glands from the sacrum bone at the pelvis to the skull. There are seven primary energy centers in the body. These seven energy centers are divided as follows: the lower four energy centers are considered 'Animal' and are located in the lower region of the spine starting at the sacrum and moving upwards to the heart, the fifth center located at the throat is considered 'Human', and the top two centers located in the skull are the 'Spiritual' centers. Paramahansa Yogananda describes the profound significance of the 'Spiritual' centers: "human beings were created by God with a unique endowment possessed by no lower forms: awakened spiritual centers of life and consciousness in the spine and brain that gives them the ability to express fully the divine consciousness and powers of the soul."[22]

Everyone is different. People have individual personalities and varying life situations. These aspects of one's being are generated by the unique conditions of each person's energy centers. Some people are born with fully open heart chakras, while others struggle with a lack of love. Some are great communicators (meaning they have a fully awakened throat energy center) but are lacking in areas that involve the other six energy centers. Everyone is dealt a different hand with varying degrees of chakra efficiency. In most people the lowest five chakras have some level of dysfunction—and virtually *no* functionality in the upper two 'Spiritual' centers. Since most people live only in 'Animal' and 'Human' consciousness, religions like Hinduism, Judaism, and Christianity have addressed this critical fault in the human condition. The story of Adam and Eve is an example that illustrates this *fall* from our spiritual selves to a state of being dominated by animalistic impulses and excessive captivation of materialism and physicality.

By ignoring our spiritual selves we have derailed our positive evolutionary path. We are out of balance with nature. As a species we have drifted away from our true, eternal, peaceful selves to a place dominated by the more troublesome and material aspects of being; a state of being that is easily overrun with overactive thinking and incessant, repetitive thoughts. The current state of the human mind creates most of the misery on Earth. Our out-of-control minds tell us we are unworthy of love, incapable of peace, and often times lead to violent, hateful, or self-destructive actions. Religions were created to address this most fundamental condition of being human.

Religions teach prayer and meditation to address the error of our false reliance on the material (physical) over the immaterial (spirit). Part of meditation is sitting quietly until you've gained some control over your thought patterns. The other equally important part of meditation is working actively to make sense of the problematic aspects of your life. Generally, most human problems reside in the lower 'Animal' aspects of consciousness where greed, lust, fear, self-loathing, envy, and hatred are generated.

The point of religion, and meditation, is to *raise* your consciousness from the lower levels to the highest spiritual levels. These higher spiritual centers, located in the skull, are where the truly transformative work happens towards gaining lasting peace of mind. Using meditation techniques developed over thousands of years, humans can literally raise their consciousness from 'Animal' to 'Human' and then to 'Spiritual' level, overcoming many of the mental and emotional hardships of human life. You can have "actual contact of God in the temple of meditation."[23] This process is known as *ascension*. Your consciousness is ascending *upwards* along the spine to the 'Spiritual' level where a direct and knowable relationship with God is available.

The energy centers responsible for generating peace of mind and accessing divinity are located in the interior recesses of the human brain and are loosely associated with the physical location of the pineal and pituitary glands. These energetic glands are so critical to knowing our spiritual selves that they play a central theme in the Bible. The termination of the Bible's "straightway path" are these glands. This straightway path, also known in the Bible as "the path of the Initiates" and "the Stairway to Heaven," is a path along the spine. At the end of this path, as we will learn in Genesis, you literally come face to face with God.

The process of raising your consciousness to spirit level can be understood with a simple diagram of Hindu thought that begins the first chapter of this book. This system of human regeneration has been known about for thousands of years, even showing up in the hieroglyphic artwork of early nomadic peoples. Hindus identified and wrote extensively about the chakras. This knowledge would have been available to the writers of Jewish and Christian scripture; who then incorporated their own ideas about the body's energy centers, repeatedly writing about them throughout the Old and New Testaments.

The first three books of the Bible: Genesis, Exodus, and Leviticus are tales of raising consciousness from the 'Animal' level to the 'Spiritual' level. Noah's ark is the perfect example: The "ark" contains humans and animals and is *raised* from the physical, material earth upwards towards Spirit by God's hand. In the process the material, physical "earth" is purified, washed clean of human impurities symbolic of the flood that washes away the "sins" of lower consciousness.

Within the first three books of the Bible are specific instructions on engaging the upper two spiritual centers—the pineal and pituitary glands. The pineal gland, as we will come to know, is the **doorway to God**. The pituitary gland is the **doorway to Enlightenment;** which in this case means an end to mental suffering—an end to incessant thinking. It's a complete rewiring of the brain.

The fall of man away from the spiritual to the physical, and the journey back to Spirit is the common theme throughout the Bible. The story repeats over and over again with different anthropomorphic characters in a repetitive mantra fashion. This repetition of truth, a technique commonly used in many of the world's sacred scriptures is "good, even necessary, for moral perception and spiritual assimilation, bringing out the meaning clearly."[24] The repetition of the story helps us to remember the lesson to be learned.

Tempest in the Cloud uses the King James Version of the Bible for its translations. It's among the least corrupted of the versions. If your Bible, for instance, replaces the word "subtil" with "craftiest" when referring to the serpent in Genesis Chapter Three, the entire essence of the universal truths the story is pointing towards has been maligned by malice or ignorance.

Tempest in the Cloud will help to demystify some of the most repeated biblical terms like *rod, bow, east wind, stranger,* and *spake*, and will also explain the difference between the terms *God, LORD,* and *Lord.* The book explores the mechanism of ascension known to Hindus as the Sanskrit word *Kundalini*. Kundalini, an energetic force within all people, is the vehicle for spiritual growth and for raising consciousness to Spirit. Kundalini is used to "awaken" the body's energy centers, ending with the pineal and pituitary glands, which is the only way of reaching the highest spiritual levels.

So let's begin our journey towards a better understanding of ourselves, and of the divine, by moving deeply into our own body.

THE BODY'S ENERGY CENTERS

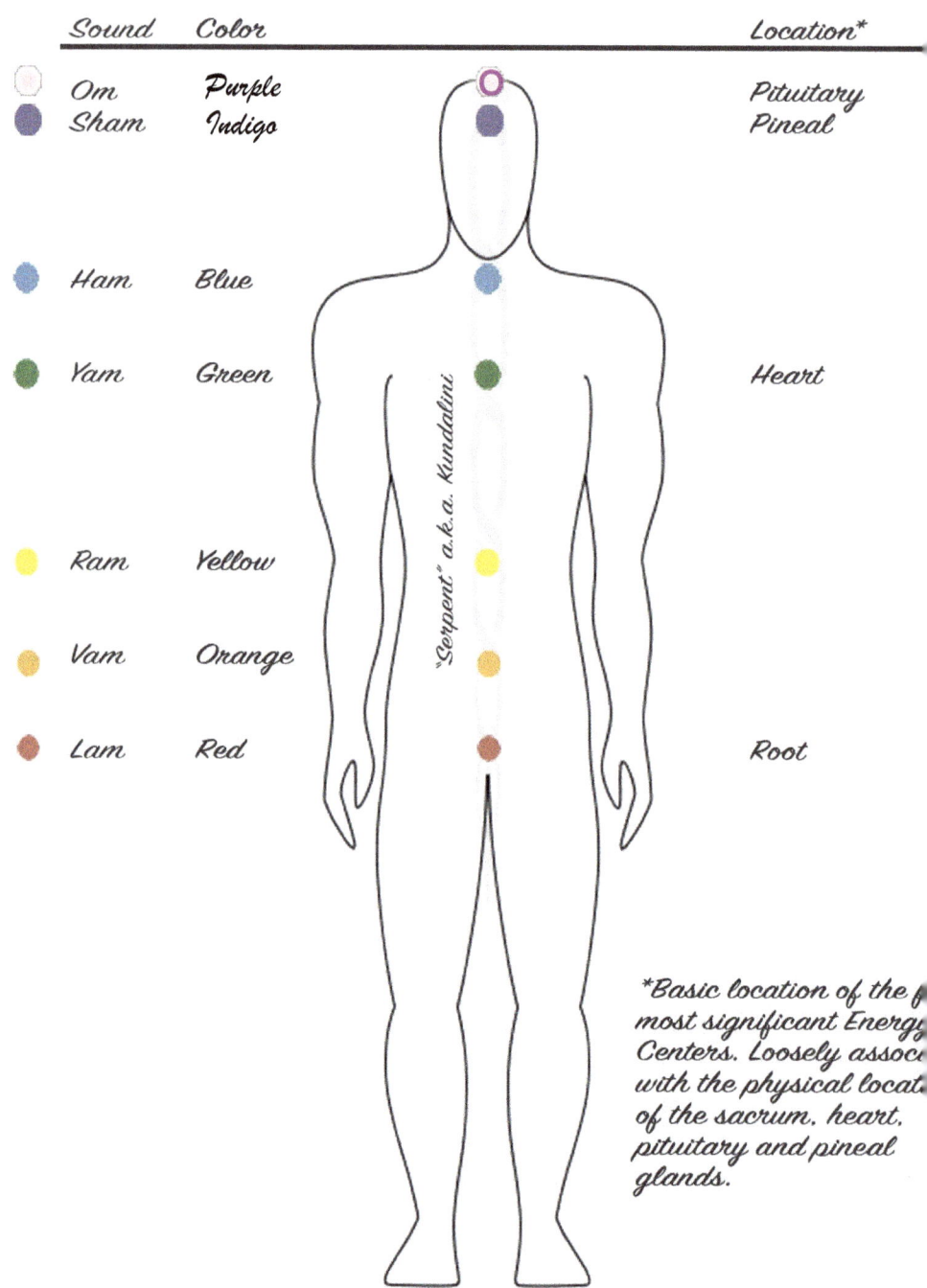

Sound	Color	Location*
Om	Purple	Pituitary
Sham	Indigo	Pineal
Ham	Blue	
Yam	Green	Heart
Ram	Yellow	
Vam	Orange	
Lam	Red	Root

"Serpent" a.k.a. Kundalini

*Basic location of the f
most significant Energy
Centers. Loosely associ
with the physical locat
of the sacrum, heart,
pituitary and pineal
glands.

GENESIS:
An Introduction to the Body's Energy Centers

The diagram of the archetypical human illustrates the general location of the body's seven primary energy centers. Every human has these energy centers. Their function is to regulate the flow of energy (consciousness) in and out of the body. The movement resembles a whirlpool or vortex and can be felt in deep meditation. The seven energy centers are associated with the body's endocrine glands. The location of the five lower centers run along the spine starting at the "cervix in women and the dormant gland called the perineal body between the urinary and excretory openings in men."[25]

It is significant to note the energy centers do not necessarily align with the physical location of particular glands. For instance, the heart energy center is actually located in the spinal cord behind the physical heart's location. Also, a major point of confusion for many is the location of the pineal and pituitary energy centers. The energy centers are *opposite* of the physical glands. Physically, the pituitary gland is lower than the pineal gland, but for the purposes of meditating on the energy centers the energetic pineal gland location is "midline of the brain directly above the spinal column," while the energetic center of the pituitary gland is "at the top of the head."[26] Therefore, the meditation focus point for the upper two glands are switched from the physical location of the two glands. This is a critical distinction missed by most references of the chakras.

The most important energy centers are the lowest *root* chakra, the *heart* chakra, and the two highest energy centers located in the skull at the pineal and pituitary glands. The pineal gland, known as the *third eye* in some cultures, is the sixth chakra and is known in yogic traditions as the "command center" that has "complete control over all the functions" of one's life.[27] The pineal gland is the literal doorway to God, and it is the reason why Christian's begin the symbolic "sign of the cross" at the location of the forehead between the eyebrows. The pituitary gland is the doorway to Enlightenment—defined here as an end to mental suffering. The pituitary gland "controls each and every gland and system in the body."[28] In the Christian Bible engaging the pituitary gland leads to the second birth where the "son of Man" becomes the "Son of God." Meaning you no longer have the mind of a mortal (material), but the mind of Spirit (immaterial).

There are three main components to our diagram of the archetypical human. First, the energy centers are color sensitive, meaning they respond to color stimulus. The colors correspond to the colors of the rainbow starting with red at the lowest center and then sequentially upwards with orange, yellow, green, blue and indigo for the pineal gland. The pituitary gland corresponds to the color purple. Second, the energy centers correlate to particular sounds known as *mantras*. When verbally repeated a mantra helps to engage, and bring vibrational focus, to the area of a particular energy center. The sound for the pineal gland, the most important energy center due to its connection to Spirit, is *Sham*. The vibrations generated by repeatedly saying the word Sham sets the stage for activating the gland. The term shaman (one who has access to the spirit side of life) most likely came from the root word Sham. While the pituitary gland's mantra of *Om* (also known as *Aum* or Amen) gets most of the attention in meditation and yoga classes, it is Sham that deserves more focus initially. Most people are nowhere near the Om level, so other than the word feeling pleasant to say, there likely isn't much happening within the pituitary gland since the pineal gland in most people has not been activated first.

The third component of our diagram is the sine wave line that passes through the seven energy centers. To Hindus this line is known as *Kundalini*. Kundalini is an energetic force that lies mostly dormant within all humans, dormant until the energy becomes activated by meditation or other spontaneous actions. Kundalini, once activated, moves along the spine purifying, widening, and enhancing the function of each energy center (chakra) as it rises upwards to the skull. Kundalini expands consciousness as it moves along each newly invigorated energy center. Kundalini floods the brain with energy activating the dormant parts of the brain. Important to note here is that each energy center is independently connected to the brain, so Kundalini does not need to awaken each center in sequential order.

Swami Satyananda Saraswati explains the awakening of the body's energy centers "as an important event in human evolution" because with the awakening of the chakras "our consciousness and our mind undergo changes. These changes have significant relevance and relationship with our day to day life." He goes on to state: "Our present state of mind is not capable of handling all the affairs of life. Our love and hatred, our relationships with people, are the consequences of the quality of our present mind. It appears our sufferings, our agonies and frustrations are not so much due to circumstances of life, but more to the responses of our mind."[29]

Kundalini is the vehicle, or the chariot, for spiritual growth. Kundalini makes its way upwards along the spine cleansing the mental and emotional parts of our being of negative life experiences (karma). There are varying views about Kundalini, but according to Satyananda Saraswati "one thing is certain—Kundalini has the ability to activate the human consciousness in such a way that a person can develop his or her most beneficial qualities, can enter a much more intimate relationship with nature and can become aware of oneness with the whole cosmos."[30]

The ascension process is a progressive spiritual awakening through the energy centers with Kundalini expanding consciousness as it makes its way towards the top of the skull. Kundalini's ultimate goal is to pierce the pineal gland—*the gateway to God*, and then the pituitary gland—*the gateway to Enlightenment*. True spiritual regeneration begins only after the top two glands have been properly engaged by divine energy. When the upper two spiritual centers are fully awakened the initiate transforms normal human consciousness into spiritual, or Christ Consciousness. Christ Consciousness, as explained by Yogananda, "can be welcomed into one's own consciousness only through the meditation-awakened straight highway of the spine."[31] The Bible's main characters, from Noah to Jesus, all used Kundalini energy to reach divinity. You must have Kundalini to enter into Eden and regain 'Spiritual' consciousness. Kundalini cannot be manipulated and is the "guardian" of the peak spiritual experience of Self-realization.

So our diagram of the prototypical human, with the location of its energy centers, has three components: sound, color, and the sine wave "serpent" that is Kundalini. Now let's look at how these elements show up in the Bible starting with Genesis Chapter

One. Genesis is a creation story that states the core "problem" with human beings is the *falling* away from Spirit. In Chapter One God creates the Universe. In Chapter Two God creates the archetypical humans Adam and Eve. The serpent is introduced in Chapter Three. That is how important the serpent (Kundalini) is to spiritual growth! The Bible says the "serpent was more subtil than any beast in the field."[32] The message here is that the serpent is **not** physical; it is energetic. The "serpent" is a metaphor. This "talking" serpent is an anthropomorphic type character. Anthropomorphism (defined as ascribing human form or attributes to a being or thing not human, particularly a deity) is a writing device used *repeatedly* throughout the Bible. The Bible is not telling us the serpent is quiet, that would be an insignificant detail to highlight, and it is not telling us the serpent is "crafty" as it has been interpreted in some versions of the Bible. The important message here is that the serpent represents "the coiled-up spinal energy"[33] located at the base of the spine. Kundalini energy—the driver of spiritual growth and the primary way to reach the Spirit level. Kundalini is the guardian of the spiritual, ascension process. If the serpent can "trick" you into "sinning" (here meaning succumbing to the illusions of the physical world) you will not be able to live in 'Spiritual' consciousness.

So far our diagram of the archetypical human and its energy centers correlates perfectly with the Bible. We have the archetypical humans in Adam and Eve and we have Kundalini as the serpent.

Next in Genesis we have Adam and Eve disobeying God and they are driven out of Eden to 'till the ground.'[34] This means humans are no longer at the 'Spiritual' level. They are now at the physical, earth level. They have fallen *downwards* to till the ground, to toil in materiality. Their consciousness is no longer at the 'Spiritual' level. Humans are now at lower consciousness. The Bible begins here with humans falling from the divine. The rest of the Bible contains stories about how to regain our spiritual consciousness, stories that illustrate the path *upward*, a return to Eden.

※

Before we continue there are a couple of significant things to know about how the Bible was written. The Bible's primary technique for telling its stories is with **symbolism**. Few of the stories and concepts are to be taken literally. For instance, the numbers 32 and 33 are of the utmost importance. God is mentioned by name 32 times in Chapter One of Genesis. Likewise, Jesus, the man, dies at the age of 33[35]. The significance of the number 32 comes from the ancient tradition of dividing the spinal column into 32 segments. Almost everything of significance in the Old Testament references the human body, as it is the human body that is the vehicle for ascension. The 32nd segment, located at the top of the spine, is the location of the pineal gland energetic center. The pineal gland is where your direct connection with God occurs, as we will learn in Chapter 32 of Genesis. The pituitary gland, which is the gland that brings about enlightenment, is energetically located at the 33rd location, or above the spinal column at the top of the skull. This also explains why freemasons, who had reached the pinnacle of masonry were called 33rd degree masons. A title that meant they had *raised* their consciousness and reached enlightenment.

Another important concept to understand about the Bible is that the human body is given east, west, north, and south coordinates. The top of the body, the head, is east, the lower section is west, the right hand is north, and the left hand is south. This is where the term *southpaw* for left-handed people originates.

As we move through the Bible we will notice that all of the "good" things happen in the east. For instance, Eden is located in the east. Meaning Eden, or the place of peace, is located in your brain. Specifically located at the pituitary gland, which we've learned is the center of enlightenment. The end of mental suffering leads to peace of mind. When Kundalini energy engages the pituitary gland during prolonged meditation you are in God's garden of peace.

Another example of the symbolism of *east* is found in the story of the Three Wise Men who visit the newly born Jesus after following a "star in the east." These same body coordinates can be found in Hinduism. Yogananda points out this similarity between Christianity and Hinduism. "In the Hindu scriptures the forehead in man is called the 'eastern' part of his body… The 'star in the east' thus symbolizes the spiritual eye in the forehead."[36]

Interestingly, we learn in Genesis that Eden is protected by cherubims and a flaming sword. Keep in mind that the Bible is profound because it is a book that is designed to describe and teach the process of ascension. Jesus ascended from human consciousness to Christ Consciousness. He did this by meditating; keeping his mind and body still. Jesus became Christ through his own body. God has built into all of us the mechanism of ascension. The point of life is to ascend to the divine as Jesus did—through his body. The Bible is a set of instructions on how to ascend as Jesus did. The stories in the Bible, particularly the Old Testament, use metaphor and anthropomorphism to conceal the instructions so that only the worthy can understand them. The stories, unmasked of metaphor, are about the human body—which is the mechanism for ascension. The cherubims in Genesis are metaphors for the brain. And the flaming sword is a metaphor for Kundalini—which has as two of its distinguishing features hot in temperature and piercing pain. The Bible states that Eden is being protected between two cherubims and a flaming sword. Eden is the pituitary gland that is located between the two halves of the human brain. The upper spiritual centers are God's garden of peace and divinity.

To further illustrate the point that the core human issue is our fall from the 'Spiritual' level down to the material level, Chapter Four of Genesis introduces two offspring of Adam and Eve. It's the birth of mankind. We learn that the two sons of Adam and Eve are named Cain and Abel and that they have jobs. Abel is a keeper of sheep and Cain is a "tiller of the ground." As we learned in Chapter Three, God banished Adam and Eve to "till the ground," meaning they are on the material, physical level—no longer of Spirit. Abel, on the other hand, is a keeper of sheep. In the Bible Jesus is compared to a shepherd, which is a metaphor for a spiritual leader tending the "flock"—people. Cain brings God the fruits of his labor and God is angry. Cain's "fruits of his labor" are his materialistic ways. God does not like Cain's attachment to the illusory physical world. Abel brings the fruits of his labor to God and God is pleased. Abel's work is spiritual in nature.

So in the story of Cain and Able we have two ways for mankind to live: physical or spiritual. Material or immaterial. So guess which way wins? Cain kills Abel. Our addiction to the material world overtakes our spiritual nature. Luckily for us, God gives mankind another chance when Adam and Eve have a third son named Seth.

Up to this point in our comparison between the diagram of the archetypical human and the Bible we have the archetypical man in Adam and we have the serpent—whose job it is to allow only the worthy (those whose consciousness is ready to rise to 'Spiritual' level) back into Eden. The only thing missing in our comparison are the body's seven energy centers. Let's look at the next story in the Bible and see if we can find any mention of the centers there.

Chapter Five of Genesis begins with Noah and his Ark. Like many of the stories in the Bible, Noah's Ark has a double meaning. There is the literal rendition of the story of God flooding the planet to get rid of evil, but the real power of the parable lies in the hidden, or esoteric, message concealed within the tale. The literal story doesn't make that much sense. The boat is too small to carry 100 animals much less two of every kind. This is a hint, a signpost, to look deeper into the story. There's much more there.

First, we learn that Noah "walked with God." He is our ideal, archetypical human. Then we learn he has three sons: Shem, Ham, and Japeth. If you recall from our diagram at the beginning of this chapter, Shem (pronounced Sham), and Ham are two of the verbal mantras for engaging the energy centers. Sham helps open the pineal gland, and Ham helps to open the throat energy center. This is not a stunning coincidence. Noah's Ark is a story about raising consciousness within the body's energy centers. The "ark" is the human body.

Along with Noah and the animals are seven people. Remember the Bible uses metaphor and anthropomorphism to conceal the truth about the ascension process that happens within your own body. Inside the ark are eight people: Noah and his seven energy centers. So in the story of Noah's Ark "people" are used to symbolize the energy centers. There's Noah, his human body (the ark), animals (lower consciousness), and his seven energy centers. That's why the ark has three levels and contains animals, humans, and a window at the top looking to heaven. The three levels symbolize the three levels of consciousness: 'Animal', 'Human,' and 'Spiritual'.

As a literal story there's not that much relevant meaning for someone living today. The flood would have happened long ago. The hidden meaning pertains to every living person today. The story of Noah's Ark is a story about *your* spiritual journey. A journey with a straightway path that has not changed in thousands of years. The esoteric story is relevant to you now.

As we move through the story we notice repeating phrases like *breath of life, lift up, nostrils, face,* and *wind.* Throughout the Bible repeating words signal for the reader to pay close attention to what's being written. Here, these repeated words are signals for us that this is an internal occurrence. It is happening within our bodies. And breath is the key. It is breath that propels the energy to where it needs to go in the body. Mostly *upwards* in our case.

In the story of Noah's Ark we are introduced to the number 40 for the first time in the Bible. The number 40 is one of the most repeated numbers in the Bible. The number 40 refers to the length of time it takes to complete the regeneration process (going from 'Animal' to 'Spiritual' consciousness) also known as being "born again." The number is simply symbolic. It doesn't mean it actually takes a set amount of time like days, months, or years to literally finish the ascension process. The number 40 is the important symbol to pay attention to. The number 40 is derived from the number of weeks in a human pregnancy—hence the "born again" birth connection.

While 40 refers to the completion of the journey from the lowest energy center to the highest at the top of the skull, it does not mean that a person is permanently enlightened as we will learn in the Bible's next book Exodus, where Moses, who finishes the journey but must repeat it when his lower consciousness fails to come under the rule, or influence, of 'Spiritual' consciousness.

Now we come to one of the most beautiful passages in the Bible.

> *God shall enlarge Japeth, and he shall dwell in the tents*
> *of Shem; and Ca'-na-an shall be his servant.*
> Genesis 9:27

This passage tells us a lot about the techniques the Bible uses to conceal messages. The passage makes little sense as it is literally written—until you decode it; then it is truly beautiful. From our diagram at the beginning of the chapter we know that Noah's "son" Shem is actually Sham the pineal gland. Noah's "son" Ham is the throat energy center. So Noah's son Japeth must be the next energy center in sequential order and that is the heart.

So let's look at the passage by removing the metaphors and replacing them with the actual meaning. "God shall enlarge Japeth" makes no sense if Japeth is a human, but as an energy center it makes perfect sense. The energy centers in our body constantly expand (open and healthy) and contract (closed and impaired). An open energy center allows more healing energy to enter into the body. God shall enlarge the *heart* is what the sentence is actually saying. The heart center is the direct pathway to the 'Spiritual' level. A healthy, expanded heart energy center is vital to making it to 'Spiritual' consciousness. "Dwell in tents" is a reference to the energy centers, so *dwell in the tents of Shem*, means to have presence and mental focus on the mantra Sham and the pineal gland. *Canaan* is a play on the word Cain, Adam and Eve's materialistic son that killed Abel. Cain stands for the physical, or man. A key technique used throughout the Bible is to have similar sounding words mean the same concept or process. So Cain and Canaan mean the same thing—physical, not spiritual. Of man, not of God.

When we rewrite the passage with the above definitions the true teaching is revealed: God shall enlarge the heart center and the heart (love) shall live in the pineal gland (Spirit) and the materialistic impulses of man shall be its (Spirit's) servant. The key to opening the pineal gland and 'Spiritual' consciousness is love. The heart's energy. The key to God is love. 'Spiritual' consciousness will rule over materialistic action. Physicality is *secondary* to Spirit. This is the true nature of humans.

The significance of this passage wouldn't be lost on the meditator who has Kundalini energy and is ready to engage the pineal gland. The heart's energy is the key to opening the pineal gland. A person in this position would engage their heart with presence and a deep sense of love. This potent energy, created and nurtured in meditation, literally streams out of the heart energy center and flows directly into the location of the pineal gland. This love energy is an integral component of opening the pineal gland to the 'Spiritual' level.

In the story of Noah's Ark, the "flood" is happening inside Noah's body. The "flood" will also happen to any initiate who is ready to meditate on the heart chakra while engaging the pineal gland with enhanced Kundalini energy. The water represents life and purification, cleansing the 'Animal' and 'Human' aspects of consciousness to the 'Spiritual' level. "A flood to destroy all flesh,"[37] the Bible states. A flood that destroys the material delusions of man, that brings about a return to spiritual consciousness.

After the story of Noah we are introduced to the biblical term *bow*. Bow is one of the most repeated words in the Old Testament signifying the importance of the word. Bow is first used in the biblical term *rain bow*. Not rainbow, but rain bow. The separation of the word rainbow into the two word rain bow sets apart and distinguishes the emphasis on the word bow. The esoteric significance of the word bow lies within the story. After the purifying "flood," which happens internally, the energy centers are expanded and operating at an increased resonance. The color sensitive energy centers beam with light. The energy centers have the same colors of light found in an actual rainbow. In your mind's eye you will see color particles flash before you. Or to use another metaphor the Bible uses, the energy centers will be like "oil for the light."[38] Brightly shining energy centers are a sign that 'Spiritual' consciousness has been achieved or close at hand.

Bow is used in different ways throughout the Old Testament. There is bow as in a rainbow, and then there is bow as in "bow and arrow." Typically the word bow is used in conjunction with a direction of up or down. When the Bible uses the word bow with the direction of up, as in a bow and arrow being pointed upwards, the biblical story being referenced is talking about consciousness moving in a positive, upwards direction. Spiritual progress is being made. If the bow in the story is pointing downwards the opposite is happening. Another way the term bow is used is in the sense of "bowing your head down." When you're in the presence of divinity, which you will be when your pineal gland is first opened, be sure to bow your head in reverence for the moment you are experiencing.

After the story of Noah's Ark concludes, Genesis goes into a long list of generations. Listing generations is a device heavily used in the Bible. When the Bible speaks of generations, it is referring to the state of your energy centers in the future. Are the positive spiritual changes you are making permanent? Or will you regress backwards to lower consciousness once again? 'Spiritual' consciousness must be maintained through effort and continued meditation. We are humans and "flesh is weak." Will we slip back into lower consciousness? Pulled down by the powerful influences of life on the earthly plane.

We can look at the example of Shem to understand how generations work in the Bible. The children of Shem are listed. Genesis 10:30 states the children "dwell on a mount in the east." The "mount" is the pineal gland. Shem (pronounced Sham) is the mantra for the pineal gland. East is the top portion of the human body, specifically the skull. You will notice right away while reading the Bible that almost all movement is up or down. The movement is along the spine. Upward movement is movement towards spiritual enlightenment. Downward movement is the soul moving towards materiality and physicality. Listed as a descendant of Shem is Abram. That means Abram is the next character in the Bible to represent the pineal gland and 'Spiritual' consciousness.

Generations highlight an important concept in the ascension process. The process is not absolute. You must actively work to maintain the progress you've made towards 'Spiritual' consciousness. The point of raising your consciousness to Spirit level is not to ignore or stifle your lower energy centers. Once you reach the initial stages of 'Spiritual' consciousness (i.e. once you've activated your pineal gland), your work is to begin to turn control of lower consciousness (the lower energy centers) over to 'Spiritual' consciousness.

After Abram the next descendent of Shem is Jacob. Jacob is famous for his ladder. The "ladder" is a metaphor for the spine. The journey Jacob is on is a journey along his spine. Jacob is on the ascension path. The journey Jacob is taking is to make the influence of his spiritual centers felt by the lower energy centers. Lower consciousness must come under the influence of 'Spiritual' consciousness.

For a real world example we can look at human sexual behavior. Before someone has made it to 'Spiritual' consciousness, while a person is still heavily influenced by lower consciousness, sex may simply be about personal gratification and lust. After making it to 'Spiritual' consciousness, sex is still allowed (as we will learn in the Bible's third book Leviticus) but sex would be more focused on mutuality, connection, and love. So the lower energy centers are not to be ignored once 'Spiritual' consciousness has been achieved. The lower energy centers are to be brought under the influence of the upper spiritual centers, specifically the pineal gland. All of the journeys in the Bible are about raising consciousness to 'Spiritual' level. These are stories told over and over again in mantra fashion to help the initiate better retain the knowledge.

A wonderful thing happens during the story of Jacob's journey. We get to Chapter 32 of Genesis. We can recall from earlier in this book that the number 32 is very significant. God is mentioned by name 32 times in the first chapter of Genesis. 32 indicates the location of the pineal gland at the upper end of the spine. When someone who is meditating successfully engages the pineal gland you literally reach the doorway to God. So now we have arrived at the revealing Chapter 32 of Genesis, can we expect to learn something profound and spectacular within the Bible at this point? In Chapter 32 we find Jacob *rising* up to a place,

> *And Jacob called the name of the place Pe-ni-el: for I have seen God face to face and my life is preserved.*[39]

"Peniel" is a direct reference to the pineal gland. Everything a seeker hopes to find is found when the pineal gland is engaged.

Is God real? You will know when you open your pineal gland. The Bible states it in clear and specific terms. Your life will be preserved and you will see God face to face. Reaching the pineal gland is the pinnacle of the human experience. What is more important than meeting God while still on Earth? This is not a metaphor. There is no hidden meaning. Open your pineal gland and meet God. This is a Universal Truth.

∞

Up to this point we've seen the Bible use anthropomorphism to symbolize the human body's energy centers in two ways. In Noah's Ark "people" were used to symbolize the seven energy centers. In the story of Jacob and his ladder a place, or "city" (Pe-ni-el) is used to symbolize the pineal gland energy center. Throughout the Bible people and cities are used metaphorically to represent the energy centers. You will notice that in almost every case the metaphors come in a set of seven (i.e the seven churches of Asia, the seven seals, the seven angels, and the seven candlesticks in the Book of Revelation).[40] When characters in the Bible are moving from city to city, or land to land, the esoteric meaning of that movement is along the spine. If the movement is upwards or to the east, then consciousness is moving towards the 'Spiritual' level.

The stories in the Bible illustrate the work to be done on the energy centers. As the characters move from one place to another they are doing the necessary inner work to heal human afflictions. The work is to meditate on one energy center and then move to another healing yourself from the afflictions associated with lower consciousness. Heal your low self-esteem, heal your greed, heal your anger, and heal your low capacity for loving. This is the work to be done. For "no spiritual progress is possible without introspection and self-study."[41]

In the next chapter of *Tempest in the Cloud* we take a look at the Bible's second book Exodus. Exodus takes a closer look at how the journey from lower consciousness to 'Spiritual' consciousness takes place. The story chronicles the journey out of "Egypt," which is a metaphor for the lowest energy centers. Why would the writers of the Bible use Egypt to symbolize the lower energy centers? Because the Jewish writers of the Old Testament were making a statement about the ancient Egyptian belief in multiple Gods, which the Jewish mystics knew was incorrect. The journey out of Egypt is symbolic of the journey out of ignorance towards enlightenment. It's an exodus from 'Animal' consciousness to 'Spiritual' consciousness. It is a common theme used throughout the Bible. God sends an initiate—Abraham, Jacob, Joseph and his coat of many colors (the multicolored energy centers), Moses, Aaron, and Jesus—to Egypt to save the "people." It is an effort to convert lower consciousness to the highest 'Spiritual' consciousness. We will also learn how Exodus gives the meditator specific instructions on how to engage the pineal gland, along with descriptions of particular breathing and visualization techniques that are to be used to have a face to face meeting with God.

EXODUS:
The Journey Out of Lower Consciousness

The Bible's first book, Genesis, starts with a creation story that illustrates the current evolutionary state of mankind. A core problem is stated that humans have incarnated onto the physical plane but have forgotten their spiritual origins. Humans are trapped in the illusion of materiality, which has led the human mind away from peace to a state of consistent turmoil. Humans are addicted to physicality at the expense of Spirit. The purpose of the biblical stories is to show the pathway back to divinity—the soul's true home. This pathway is called ascension or resurrection. Human consciousness is *ascending* to spiritual consciousness.

The Bible's second book, Exodus is another story about raising consciousness from 'Animal' and 'Human' to 'Spiritual' consciousness. Exodus moves deeply into the ascension process. The story is an exodus out of the grip of the materialistic influences of our lives and towards a shift to the immaterial, spiritual reality that is at the core of our being. The story of Moses, the main protagonist in Exodus, is a story of spiritual renewal.

The profundity of the Bible doesn't rely on the fact of whether or not Moses actually existed as a historical person, the profoundness of the Bible is found in the example the characters are illustrating in regards to the ascension process; a process which is available to every human regardless of any particular historical time period. The Bible remains significant and relevant because it is not simply a story about people who lived thousands of years ago, but a book that gives instructions for the modern person on how they can have a personal, direct, and knowable connection with God.

Exodus illustrates how God uses divine energy, known as Kundalini, to help humans out of the snare of the sorrows of life. The book is a sophisticated and complex story about this divinely driven journey to spiritual consciousness which has at its ending the characteristics of Enlightenment and Self-Realization; an end to mental suffering and the realization that we are immaterial souls temporarily occupying a physical body. It is an end to the false illusion of the physical world. Exodus ends with a series of instructions on how this journey to God and Enlightenment is to be taken. It is specifically written for the person ready to engage the spiritual centers within the human body located at the pineal and pituitary glands. These glands are to be engaged with inner work that includes prayer, meditation, and Kundalini.

Exodus begins in Egypt. Remember the writers of the Bible use **symbolism** to mask meaning so that only the prepared initiate is able to decipher the hidden messages within the story. To uncover the true essence of the Bible it should be read like a poem. In Exodus, Egypt symbolizes lower consciousness. Lower consciousness is the energy within humans that generates and regulates aspects of our humanity such as greed, fear, hatred, and self-esteem. So the story of Exodus is a story about how to overcome the problematic aspects of lower consciousness. It's an exodus away from materiality.

Exodus Chapter 1 begins,
> *Now these are the names of the children of Is'-ra-el, which came into E'-gypt; every man and his household came with Jacob.*

Jacob is a descendant of Shem. Shem we know is symbolizing the mantra *Sham,* which opens the pineal gland—the doorway to God. So the "children of Israel" came with Jacob. The children of Israel, also referred here by "every man and his household," is symbolizing the body's energy centers under the control of 'Spiritual' consciousness. The story is telling us that "the children of Israel" are the body's energy centers that have been transformed, placed under the rule or influence of the spiritual glands.

Exodus Chapter 1:5 and 1:6,
> *And all the souls that came out of the loins of Ja'-cob were seventy souls: for Jo'-seph was in E'-gypt already. And Jo'-seph died, and all his brethren, and all that generation.*

In Genesis, Jacob and Joseph make the journey to Egypt to bring their lower consciousness under the rule of 'Spiritual' consciousness. In this passage the scene is being set for the rest of Exodus. We are at the starting point of the story. We are in the state of Enlightenment and Self-Realization. In Exodus Chapter 1:7 we learn,
> *And the children of Is'-ra-el were fruitful, and increased abundantly, and multiplied, and waxed exceedingly mighty; and the land was filled with them.*

This passage is telling us that all of the body's energy centers are under the direction of the spiritual centers. All centers are working together. This is the optimal state of a human being.

> In Exodus Chapter 1:8 we are introduced to the king of Egypt.
> *Now there arose up a new king over E'-gypt, which knew not Jo'-seph.*

The "king of Egypt" represents the lower energy centers. Joseph, a descendent of Shem, symbolizes 'Spiritual' consciousness. So the king of Egypt does not know 'Spiritual' consciousness. This passage is telling us that there has been a negative change in consciousness in the story. We have shifted from 'Spiritual' consciousness to lower consciousness.

> Exodus Chapter 1:9
> *And he said unto his people, Behold, the people of the children of Is'-ra-el are more and mightier than we;*

Spiritual consciousness is more powerful than lower consciousness.

> Exodus Chapter 1:10
> *Come on, let us deal wisely with them; lest they multiply, and it come to pass, that, when there falleth out any war, they join also unto our enemies, and fight against us, and so get them up out of the land.*

The "king of Egypt," (lower consciousness) does not want to come under the rule of higher consciousness (the children of Israel). Human life would be much more joyful if it was easy to live in spiritual consciousness away from the pull of materiality.

The lower four energy centers have an extremely strong hold on human consciousness. This energy, the densest part of our being, keeps us stuck in physicality. It's very easy to succumb to the delusions of the physical world. As an example in human behavior, this could show up as someone succumbing to temptation even though they know better. Doing something you know is wrong, but not having the willpower to change your behavior. This passage is illustrating the primary error in the human mind: An over-reliance of the physical over the immaterial (spirit). We would rather buy that shiny new car than donate our time to feeding the hungry. This is not a judgment about morality or ethics. No one is saying not to buy and enjoy the car. Just don't put your happiness into something that will fall apart and decay. All material structures disintegrate. Place your happiness on the immaterial aspects of life. Love. Compassion. Faith. Beauty. These things live as conscious energy forever. The above biblical passage is acknowledging that the pull of materiality is strong, but with cultivation (prayer, meditation, and presence) spiritual consciousness is stronger.

> Exodus Chapter 1:11
>
> *Therefore they (the Egyptians) did set over them (the children of Israel) taskmasters to afflict their burdens. And they built for Pha'-roah treasure cities, Pi'-thom and Ra-am'-ses.*

The king of Egypt (lower consciousness) has overtaken spiritual consciousness. Human afflictions (i.e. greed, lust, hatred…) have disrupted the peace of mind that comes with higher consciousness. The lower energy centers are symbolized here as "treasure cities." The term treasure symbolizes materiality. The acute observer will notice the similarities of the mantra *ram* that opens the third chakra (from our diagram at the beginning of the first chapter of this book) and the "city" Ra-am'-ses.

> Exodus Chapter 1:13 & 1:14
> *And the E-gyp'-tians made the children of Is'-ra-el to serve with rigour: And they made their lives bitter with hard bondage, in mortar, and in brick, and in all manner of service in the field: all their service, wherein they made them serve, was in rigour.*

The Egyptians are enslaving the children of Israel. Lower consciousness is obscuring spiritual consciousness thereby making life hard. Spirit is being ignored at the expense of materiality (brick and mortar). Like Adam, Eve, and Cain, the children of Israel are made to "service in the field," to toil in physicality. In this portion of the story Exodus, the king of Egypt is keeping the "people" in bondage. He sets over them "taskmasters" to afflict them with their burdens. The "people" (human consciousness) are trapped in the pain generated in the lower energy centers. We have become overwhelmed with the desires, influences, and heartaches of living in a world dominated by materialism. Pain that leads to incessant, negative thoughts along with mental and emotional distress. Our negative thought patterns create our own hardships making life harder than it needs to be. To rise once again to spiritual consciousness we must break the binds that keep us bounded to physical delusion. "Egypt," the lower consciousness, is the generator of human mental suffering and must be brought under the influence of the 'Spiritual' energy centers.

> Exodus Chapter 2:23

> *And it came to pass in process of time. That the king of E'-gypt died: and the children of Is'-ra-el sighed by reason of the bondage, and they cried, and their cry came up unto God by reason of the bondage.*

In time, with God's help, the person who addresses their issues involving lower consciousness (i.e. greed, hate, lust...) will be released from the mental and emotional toll these things have on the human mind. In Buddhism there is a famous saying for this idea: Life is suffering. The release of this suffering is through meditation, prayer, and presence. By actively addressing the problematic areas of your life you lessen the degree of suffering. This is the inner work that humanity must do individually and collectively.

Exodus Chapter 2:24 & 2:25
> *And God heard their groaning, and remembered his covenant with A'-bra-ham, with I'-saac, and with Ja'-cob. And God looked upon the children of Is'-ra-el, and God had respect unto them.*

Abraham, Isaac, and Jacob are all descendants of Shem. They are symbolic of the pineal gland. God's "covenant" is the pineal gland. The pineal gland is the way to know God directly. As we learned in Genesis Chapter 32, when you fully open the pineal gland your life is preserved. The pineal gland is God's commitment to humanity that there is a way out of suffering.

Exodus Chapter 3:7
> *And the LORD said, I have surely seen the affliction of my people which are in E'-gypt, and have heard their cry*

> *by reason of their taskmasters; for I know their sorrows.*

The "taskmasters" are our own thoughts, emotions, and distractions. God understands, and has compassion, for the human mind's propensity for strife.

> Exodus Chapter 3:8
> *And I am come down to deliver them out of the hands of the E-gyp'-tians, and to bring them up out of that land unto a good land, and a large, unto a land flowing with milk and honey; unto a place of the Ca'na'an-ites, and the Hit'-tites, and the Am'-o-rites, and the Per-iz'-zites, and the Hi'-vites, and the Jeb'-u-sites.*

God will deliver us out of the debilitating grip of lower consciousness and raise us to higher spiritual consciousness. The term *land* is again used to symbolize the seven energy centers. The terms *milk and honey* are used to describe the upper energy centers that make life sweeter and more nourishing. The upper energy centers are the centers of human health and well-being. The six names in the last part of the passage symbolize the body's lower six energy centers that must be passed through to achieve a state of 'Spiritual' consciousness.

> Exodus Chapter 3:19
> *And I am sure that the king of E'-gypt will not let you go, no, not by a mighty hand.*

God knows the strong influence of the material world on the human mind. It is not easy to raise your consciousness from the lower levels up to spirit level. The illusion of the physical world is hard to overcome. Lower consciousness has a stronghold on humanity.

> Exodus Chapter 3:20
> *And I will stretch out my hand, and smite E'-gypt with all my wonders which I will do in the midst thereof; and after that he will let you go.*

God will help us overcome lower consciousness. This is the ascension (or resurrection) process. The spiritual centers (the pineal and pituitary glands) can only be opened with God's help. The "wonders" God will do in front of you include Kundalini and the events that happen when the pineal gland is opened known as Passover. The term *midst* is heavily used in the Bible. It has two meanings. One of the meanings is literal: these things will happen in front of you. You will know when it is happening. The Passover event that happens when you open your pineal gland is unmistakable. The second meaning of the word is a play on the word *mist*. The literal Passover event that happens when the pineal gland is engaged with Kundalini energy is accompanied with a presence of mist. The physical space you occupy during the pineal gland meditation will fill with mist. Literally.

This first part of Exodus explains the basics of the ascension process. The problem: Humans are stuck in the illusion of the material world, and that leads to mental and emotional strife. The solution: Raise your consciousness to the spirit level by doing the necessary inner work through meditation, prayer, and divine guidance. God knows this will be a difficult journey. Anyone trying to overcome the traumatic experiences of loss of love, betrayal, or abandonment knows how difficult it can be to move beyond the grief, fear, and anger that can arise from those types of situations.

The journey of raising consciousness to the 'Spiritual' level in order to find lasting peace of mind is the primary theme of the Bible. It is also the theme of the story of Moses. The story of Moses begins with several terms that underscore the issue at hand. Terms like *vain, sorrow, oppression, burdens,* and *afflictions* bring focus to the unhappiness and hardships of living under the rule of lower consciousness. In Chapter 3 of Exodus we find Moses in the company of the LORD and the appearance of a flaming bush. The flaming bush that does not get consumed is a metaphor for Kundalini. Kundalini is the flame inside our body that does not burn us. It is God's divine energy. The word *rod* is also repeatedly used in Exodus and the Bible. Rod is a metaphor for the spine. When God gives Moses a rod that turns into a serpent the story is letting us know that Moses has Kundalini energy. The precursor for engaging the spiritual energy centers at the pineal and pituitary glands. Kundalini is the vehicle for spiritual rejuvenation.

So we have Moses as our archetypical human. He has been given Kundalini energy by God and is now on the spiritual journey towards Enlightenment and Self-Realization. Moses, like all human beings, is not perfect. So God sends his brother Aaron to help him on his journey. A point should be made here about the relationships of the characters in the Bible. Is Aaron actually Moses' brother? Or is Aaron an aspect of Moses, a quality Moses lacks, that God provides to Moses so that he can complete the ascension process to spiritual liberation? In Exodus Chapter 4:10 "And Mo'-ses said unto the LORD, I am not eloquent, neither heretofore, nor since thou hast spoken unto thy servant: but I am slow of speech and of slow tongue." Moses tells God he is not very good at communication, which would be the energy center located at the throat. We know that the spiritual journey involves meditation and that doing the inner work on ourselves is a solo journey. So Aaron may not be a real person. Perhaps he is an anthropomorphic, metaphorical gift from God to heal Moses' faulty throat chakra. An aspect of Moses consciousness that needs healing. Don't get too caught up in the relationships in the Bible. The action between the characters is the significant part of the teaching. Remember that the story is about *your* spiritual journey. The Bible is a manual for *your* human body. Pay attention to what is happening with the characters, not who they may or may not have been in the historical past.

You will notice while reading the Bible the words God, LORD, and Lord used throughout. They don't mean the same thing. God is the creator of the Universe. LORD is the part of God that shows up in *you*. You will literally experience this when your pineal gland is activated by Kundalini. Lord is a term that describes someone who has activated their pineal gland. Jesus became Lord when he raised his human consciousness to Christ Consciousness.

So LORD (God in Moses) says to Aaron in Exodus Chapter 4:27,

Go into the wilderness and meet Moses.

Moses is with God in meditation or prayer. The "wilderness" is a metaphor for lower consciousness. It's where 'Animal' consciousness lives. Wilderness also has the connotation of silence. It is quiet reflection in deep meditation that transforms lower consciousness into spiritual consciousness. Moses, with the help of Aaron, is ready to take his journey out of Egypt—out of the wilderness—out of lower consciousness.

So we have Moses and Aaron about to go on a spiritual journey. The same one that is repeatedly described throughout the Bible. God has given both Moses and Aaron rods that turn into serpents. Meaning both Moses and Aaron have Kundalini energy running up their spines. The journey begins in Egypt. The "people" Moses and Aaron are sent to save are not real people. They are the human aspects of Moses that need to come under the spiritual influence of the pineal gland, that once fully awakened has the potential of transforming human thoughts and behaviors away from animalist instincts to a higher-order functioning based on spiritual aspirations. Greed turns into sharing, hate turns into love, jealousy turns into admiration, fear turns into faith, and doubt turns into optimism.

These soul transforming occurrences happen through meditation. When LORD tells Moses to "rise up early in the morning" in Exodus Chapter 8:20, LORD is referring to meditation or prayer. Throughout the Bible we are reminded to sit silently or to be still. In the book of Psalms we are repeatedly told to meditate, "Be still and know that I am God." 46:10

So Moses and Aaron are on the ascension journey. They are taking the "straightway path" from lower consciousness to spiritual consciousness. A path that runs along the spine from the lowest root chakra, located at at the sacrum, to the crown chakra at the top of the head. Moses and Aaron are starting in Egypt, the lowest energy centers. The journey is a battle to overcome the influences of the lower consciousness. Lower consciousness, the part of the human psyche that generates thoughts and emotions such as self-hatred, envy, and conceit, is extremely hard to overcome. A serious meditation and prayer regimen, along with divine guidance, is required. Lower consciousness will not give up control easily.

Exodus Chapter 8:32

And Pha'-raoh hardened his heart at this time also, neither would he let the people go.

Lower consciousness will not easily let go of control. The influences of the material world have a strong grip on the human mind. The illusion of physicality is enticing. A clue is given in this passage on the how the ascension journey must be taken; it must be taken with an open heart.

In Exodus Chapter 9:4 we see progress for Moses and Aaron on the ascension path. At this point in the story we have LORD (God in Moses) interacting with animals.

And the LORD shall sever between cattle of Is'-ra-el and the cattle of E'gypt: and there shall nothing die of all that is the children of Is'-ra-el.

So here the Bible is pointing to a critical distinction about the lower energy centers—the difference in the state of mind between the lower 'Animal' energy centers under the influence of lower consciousness (cattle of Egypt) AND the lower energy centers under the influence of 'Spiritual' consciousness (cattle of Israel). The cattle of Egypt shall die, and the cattle of Israel shall live. The point of the ascension process is to bring your lower consciousness, the lower 'Animal' energy centers under the rule of the 'Spiritual' centers.

Exodus Chapter 9:6

And the LORD did that thing on the morrow, and all the cattle of E'-gypt died; but of the cattle of the children of Is'-ra-el died not one.

The "cattle of the children of Israel" did not die. Meaning the animal instincts under the rule of the body's spiritual centers have not died. The goal of the ascension process is not to "kill," or ignore, the lowest energy centers. 'Animal' consciousness under the rule, or influence, of 'Spiritual' consciousness is the goal. This is an important distinction that is generally misunderstood in religion. The spiritual journey is not trying to eliminate everything 'Animal' and 'Human' about us. Simply that these aspects of consciousness should be aligned with spiritual goals based on mutuality, compassion, and love. The goal here is to raise consciousness to the highest ideals possible. Not perfection. Not asexual. Not obsessive. Not judgmental. Just our best selves; as good as we can be.

Exodus Chapter 9:13
And the LORD said unto Mo'-ses, Rise up early in the morning, and stand before Pha'-raoh, and say unto him, Thus saith the LORD God of the He'-brews, Let my people go, that they may serve me.

LORD (God showing up in Moses) tells Moses to rise up early in the morning. This is telling us that Moses is in prayer or meditation. Moses is standing before the Egyptian Pharoah, which means Moses is confronting his lower consciousness. The Pharoah symbolizes spiritual ignorance. "Let my people go," means to transform 'Human' consciousness to 'Spiritual' consciousness. This is the transformation that will serve you, and humanity. Transform lower consciousness to spiritual consciousness and your life will be saved. Overcome the mental anguish that comes from lower consciousness and you will know peace. That is what serves Moses, and will serve anyone who takes the ascension journey.

Exodus Chapter 9:23

> *And Mo'-ses stretched forth his rod toward heaven: and the LORD sent thunder and hail, and the fire ran along upon the ground; and the LORD rained hail upon the land of E'-gypt.*

Moses raising his rod toward heaven is a reference to Kundalini. Kundalini is God's energy that runs along the spine. Kundalini is an extremely powerful energy that burns up lower consciousness. In the Eastern religions one might say it this way: *Kundalini burns up karma.* Thunder, hail, and fire are all descriptive terms that characterize the actual sensations someone who has Kundalini energy would feel inside their body as this incredibly powerful energy works its way up the spine.

The battles in the Bible are internal occurrences. The battles are happening inside your body. That is how consciousness evolves. Meditation is an arduous undertaking. No one goes through a radical spiritual transformation without dealing with major mental and emotional issues. Overcoming the sorrows of life is not an easy task.

As the battle rages in Exodus (the battle to put lower consciousness under the influence of spiritual consciousness) the Bible gives clues on how this battle should be approached with the repetition of several key words. Words like *humble* and *presence* point to humility and meditation. Put your ego aside when you're doing spiritual work so that you don't fall into the trap of *spiritual materialism.* If you begin to feel superior to others because you have discovered the way to enlightenment, you have traded one snare for another. You are not making progress and have fallen back to lower consciousness. The term *east wind* is a reference to Kundalini, the moving energy inside you that feels like moving air. A "wind" that comes from heavenly sources.

In Exodus Chapter 12 we have the terms *sacrificial lamb, burning with fire, Passover, unleavened bread,* and the *meditation of seven days*. These terms refer to meditation and are not to be taken literally. The animal sacrifices in the Bible are metaphorical. The "sacrificial lamb" is symbolic of the state of the meditative mind. Lamb is symbolic of "innocence, meekness, and loyalty."[42] The way to overcome lower consciousness is with *self-sacrifice* (i.e. service to others). "Burning with fire" points to heated Kundalini energy. It is negative thinking that must be "burned" up with Kundalini. "Unleavened bread" is a metaphor for a quieted mind. Thoughts have not risen. "Passover" happens to the meditator who has opened their pineal gland with the help of Kundalini and divine guidance. God literally passes over the initiate resetting and purifying the body's energy centers. It is the moment described in Genesis Chapter 32 when Jacob sees God face to face. This is also the moment the Holy Ghost enters into your body. The Holy Ghost is not already within all humans. The Holy Ghost is within you once you've opened your pineal gland. The "meditation of seven days" is the meditation to open your pineal gland. The seven portion of the title is referring to the seven energy centers.

Another term repeated throughout the Bible is the word *stranger*. Stranger refers to someone who has completed the "seven-day meditation" to open the pineal gland, but then regresses so that the lower energy centers fail to feel the influence of the newly awakened spiritual center. That person has reached 'Spiritual' consciousness, but then returned to 'Animal' and 'Human' consciousness. Moses is initially a stranger because his lower consciousness, that is his "people" in Egypt, reject the rule of 'Spiritual' consciousness. A stranger becomes *estranged* from the Holy Ghost until the spiritual centers gain control of the lower consciousness. More meditation must be done.

It is significant to pause here and let the above explanations sink into your consciousness. In Western culture the Bible has been misunderstood for so long that it may seem incredulous to believe what actually happens in the ascension process. Raising consciousness to 'Spirit' level *is* the point of human life. Raising consciousness *is* the point of the Bible. Meditation and prayer is the way to higher consciousness. Kundalini is God's energy and it is the mechanism for accessing the spiritual centers.

When the Bible is taught literally the significance and sacredness of the teaching is lost. How many lives have been squandered by the false teaching of the Bible? How much better off would humanity be if people had understood the process it takes to reach Spirit? Let this sink into your awareness. You don't have to believe every word that is written in this book. Once you begin to seriously work on your inner issues through a disciplined meditation practice you will experience these things on your own and you will know it to be the truth. Don't try to intellectualize this book. Do your inner work and you will know by experience. You don't need a church or a pastor or a guru. If you find enlightened help it will certainly help you avoid some pitfalls along the way. But if you never find an appropriate human guide do not fret. God is waiting for you. God is waiting for you and will come to you directly. And you will be guided by divine sources on your journey. You will not be on this journey alone. That is the message of the Bible. This journey may happen very quickly for you. Start preparing now. Begin the work on your inner issues.

Exodus Chapter 13:9
> *And it shall be for a sign unto thee upon thine hand, and for a memorial between thine eyes, that the LORD's*

> *law may be in thy mouth: for with a strong hand hath the LORD brought thee out of E'-gypt.*

Between your eyes is the pineal gland. God, with a strong hand, will help lift you out of lower consciousness. Away from the negative consequences of living a life of delusion stuck in materiality.

Exodus Chapter 14:21 Moses leaves Egypt through the Red Sea.
> *And Mo'-ses stretched out his hand over the sea; and the LORD caused the sea to go back by a strong east wind all that night, and made the sea dry land, and the waters were divided.*

The Red sea is a metaphor for the root energy center that is associated with the color red. The strong east wind is a metaphor for Kundalini. Kundalini is the vehicle for raising consciousness to the 'Spiritual' level.

Exodus Chapter 14:22
> *And the children of Is'-ra-el went into the midst of the sea upon the dry ground: and the wall unto them on their right hand and on their left.*

In the meditation of seven days that leads to the opening of the pineal gland you will most likely be meditating *lying down*. Particularly if you have a tall or bulky body that can't easily maintain a sitting position for the length of time necessary to complete the seven day meditation. When you're lying down your hands will be at your side. In Eastern traditions this pose is called *dead man's pose.* Kundalini (the east wind) will be flowing from your root chakra (the Red sea) and the wall of "water" (oxygenated energy) will literally be flowing between your right hand and left. Notice here the emphasis on right hand. Right hand, as in the "the right hand of God," is used repeatedly in the Bible. When you open your pineal gland the Holy Spirit enters into your right hand and becomes an internal guide helping you along the ascension process.

The above biblical passage is so important that it is repeated again in Chapter 14:29.

> *But the children of Is'-ra-el walked upon dry land in the midst of the sea; and the waters were a wall unto them on their right hand, and on their left.*

At this point in Exodus Moses is in the process of leaving lower consciousness. He is transforming his soul from 'Animal' and 'Human' consciousness to 'Spiritual' consciousness. This is showing up as a journey out of Egypt and a movement upwards towards a "tabernacle" where Moses will find God.

Exodus Chapter 16
> *And they took their journey from E'-lim, and all the congregation of the children of Is'-ra-el came unto the wilderness of Sin… and the whole congregation…. murmured against Mo'-ses and Aa'-ron in the wilderness… And the children of Is'-ra-el said unto them, Would to God we had died by the hand of the LORD in the land of E'-gypt… for ye have brought us forth into this wilderness, to kill this whole assembly with hunger.*

This passage shows how difficult it is to raise consciousness.

Even once we are free of the influences of the lowest energy center consciousness (i.e. we've moved beyond the negative impulses of the root chakra) our willpower is still not strong enough to overcome the pull of 'Animal' consciousness. The journey to 'Spiritual' consciousness is not easy. At this point in Exodus, the "people" still do not have faith in Moses and Aaron.

The rest of Exodus Chapters 16 and 17 illustrates the continuing journey out of the "wilderness of Sin" upwards to mount Sinai (the spiritual centers). We find two periods of time mentioned in Chapter 16. We have six days of gathering bread and then resting on the seventh day. This period of time is symbolic of the seven energy centers. The story is telling us we are moving along the six lower energy centers towards the final energy center located at the crown of the skull. Then we have the forty years it takes for the "children of Israel" to get to the "borders of the land of Ca'-na-an." The "forty" number symbolizes the entire journey from the root chakra to the crown chakra. The "borders of the land of Canaan" is the border between 'Human' consciousness and 'Spiritual' consciousness (i.e. we are moving from the lower energy centers to the top two energy centers).

Exodus Chapter 18:13-14

And it came to pass on the morrow, That Mo'-ses sat to judge the people: and the people stood by Mo'-ses from the morning unto the evening. And when Mo'-ses father in law saw all that he did to the people, he said, What is this thing that thou doest to the people? Why sittest thou thyself alone, and the people stand by thee from morning unto even?

Moses is sitting in meditation. Notice the contradiction in

the passage. Moses is alone AND all the people are standing by him. This contradiction is a signpost to look closer at the passage. Moses is alone. The "people" are not actual people. The "people" are aspects of Moses' own consciousness that must be healed to make it to 'Spiritual' consciousness. The journey Moses is on is *internal.* He is meditating on his own human traits; emotions, biases, and frailties—to heal his lower consciousness. It is the weaknesses of Moses own humanness that needs to be healed. You may be surprised to learn that this is the case in many of the journeys in the Bible. The characters are healing their own human faults. That is how you become enlightened. You heal *your own* frailties and faults.

> Exodus Chapter 18:18
> *Thou wilt surely wear away both thou, and this people that is with thee: for this thing is too heavy for thee; thou art not able to perform it thyself alone.*

Moses' "father in law" is telling him that the inner work he is doing will wear on him and the "people." This is an acknowledgement that the inner work Moses is doing (and that we all must do) is very difficult. We can't do it alone. We need help.

> Exodus Chapter 18:19-20
> *Hearken now unto my voice, I will give thee council, and God shall be with thee: Be thou for the people to God-ward that thou mayest bring the causes unto God. And thou shalt teach them ordinances and laws, and shalt show them the way wherein they must walk, and do the work they must do.*

God will help us do the inner work that must be done. There is virtually no chance of advancing to 'Spiritual' consciousness until the inner work of making sense of our conflicts and afflictions is addressed.

Exodus Chapter 18:23
If thou shalt do this thing, and God command thee so, then thou shalt be able to endure, and all this people shall also go to their place in peace.

Do your inner work. God commands it to be done. If you work on your life's problems diligently then you will be able to endure the arduousness of the work. The reward of doing inner work is peace of mind. Notice the word *endure*, it is often repeated in the Bible. The process of regeneration (resurrection) is difficult. Working on our emotions can be grueling. Kundalini can be physically painful. The power of the body's energy system purifying the chakras is not for the faint of heart. The quickly moving energy can be a challenge to handle for even the toughest among us. Endure the unpleasant memories that need to be healed. Endure the physical, mental, and emotional stress of working on your inner issues. The healing process is rigorous but necessary for the radical transformation of the soul that comes with the regeneration process.

Exodus Chapter 19 is subtitled "Meeting God at Mount Sinai." Mount Sinai is a metaphor for the pineal gland. The pineal gland is where you literally meet God.

Exodus Chapter 19:11,
And be ready against the third day: for the third day

> *the LORD will come down in the sight of all the people upon the mount Si'-nai.*

While in meditation, Moses will bring his presence to the "mount" (pineal gland). The "people" have been brought out of Egypt (lower consciousness) so they are considered "purified," (nearing the 'Spiritual' level). Moses has healed his 'Animal' and 'Human' thoughts and behaviors and is ready to connect with God at the pineal gland. The "third" day is referring to the Father, the Son, and the Holy Ghost. When the pineal gland is activated there is a union of all three. A union of body, mind, and spirit is another way of symbolizing the number three.

Exodus Chapter 19:13
> *There shall not an hand touch it, but he shall surely be stoned, or shout through; whether it be beast or man, it shall not live: when the trumpet soundeth long, they shall come up to the mount.*

The LORD gives a warning that neither beast nor man shall go to the mount, or they shall not live. You can not have 'Animal' or 'Human' consciousness (thoughts) while meditating on the mount (pineal gland) or the experience will end (die). When the trumpet sounds long is a reference to the audible sound the pineal gland makes when it is hit with an enhanced, prolonged flow of Kundalini energy.

Exodus Chapter 19:14
> *And Mo'-ses went down from the mount unto the people and sanctified the people; and they washed their clothes.*

Moses has purged himself of 'Animal' and 'Human' consciousness. He is in a meditative state of 'Spiritual' consciousness. Moses is ready to meet God.

> Exodus Chapter 18:16
> *And it came to pass on the third day in the morning that there were thunders and lightnings, and a thick cloud upon the mount, and the voice of the trumpet exceeding loud; so that all the people that was in the camp trembled.*

Moses has successfully engaged his pineal gland during an intense meditation. Thunder and lightning symbolize enhanced Kundalini energy. A cloud will be seen both in the mind's eye and with the physical eyes. The pineal gland will hiss loudly. This experience is an earth-shattering event that will leave you trembling. Chapter 19 ends with the repetition of the words *spake* and *charge*. Spake is a play on the word spark. As is the word charge. The story is telling us that the opening of the spiritual centers is an energetic occurrence. Kundalini energy is striking the pineal gland in order to "charge" it.

> Exodus Chapter 20:20
> *And Mo'-ses said unto the people, Fear not: for God is come to prove you, and that his fear may be before your faces, that ye sin not.*

God will come "before your faces."

In Chapter 20 of Exodus we get to one the most controversial sections of the Bible. The section is subtitled *Ten Commandments for Israel*. We are at God's Ten Commandments. Up until this point, the *entire* Bible has been about raising consciousness to the 'Spiritual' level. Each story in Genesis, and each chapter in Exodus, has built up to the point we've just reached where Moses meditates on the pineal gland and sees God face to face. Next, the Old Testament introduces rules "for Israel." "Israel" we know symbolizes 'Spiritual' consciousness. So these are rules for people to live by to achieve higher consciousness. These are "the laws of bodily and mental discipline and meditation."[43] To keep the glands (energy centers) healthy and functioning at this higher resonance, there are considerations to keep in mind. This is the esoteric meaning of the Ten Commandments.

Let's take a closer look at some of the commandments: First, worship, or love God. That is a prerequisite for opening both the heart chakra and the pineal gland. Love God means to live in God's love. Keep your heart energy center open. Next, let's look at the commandment to remember the Sabbath. The Sabbath, or seventh day, is talking about the seventh gland: the pituitary gland.

> Exodus Chapter 20:8-10
> *Remember the sabbath day, to keep it holy. Six days shalt thou labour, and do all thy work: But the seventh day is the sabbath of the LORD thy God: in it thou shalt not do any work;*

The Bible is profound because it is teaching us how to return to our spiritual roots. This route to 'Spiritual' consciousness happens within our bodies and ends with a state of enlightenment when the *pituitary* gland is fully engaged. The only way to access the pituitary gland is with silence. We gain silence in our minds with deep meditation. This also explains the passage in Revelation

Chapter 8 "And when he had opened the seventh seal, there was silence in heaven about the space of half and hour." Open the seventh "seal" (the seventh energy center, the pituitary gland) and there will be silence. The silence is your quieted mind. It is the end of mental noise that leads to enlightenment. So when the Bible talks about doing work in six days it means to do the active *inner* work that needs to be done to heal our lower chakras. Contemplate on your personal issues. The pituitary gland can only be activated with prolonged silence.

The other commandments also are referring to the body's energy centers. Remember, your energy centers are *everything* about you. The energy centers are the point of contact where God enters into your body! There is *nothing* more important to your life than the health of your energy centers. Honor your energy centers. Give them presence and health. Do not kill your energy centers. Honor the role each one plays in your life. When the Bible mentions an "ox" or an "ass" when talking about the commandments, the story is talking about 'Animal' consciousness, or your lower energy centers. In Leviticus we learn that if you inadvertently break a commandment the remedy is to meditate. You cannot kill someone and then go meditate and be done with it. If you inadvertently "kill" a chakra by not giving it your full attention, you meditate on it by giving presence to it. You bring the energy center back to "life" (health) by bringing *presence* to it.

Immediately after the commandments the Bible returns to the place we left off in Exodus Chapter 19. The stories in the Old Testament are *one* continuous train of thought. In Exodus Chapter 18, the passage that immediately follows the commandment about not coveting your neighbor's "house" or "ox," the Bible repeats the passage from Chapter 19:16,

Exodus Chapter 20:18/20

> *And all the people saw the thunderings, and the lightnings, and the noise of the trumpet, and the mountain smoking: and when the people saw it, they removed, and stood afar off. And Mo'-ses said unto the people, Fear not: for God is come to prove you, and that his fear may be before your faces*

The commandments are bracketed by the events that lead up to the opening of the pineal gland. The commandments "for Israel" are the rules for healthy, spiritually influenced chakras.

Up to this point each of the stories in the Bible are talking about the journey to 'Spiritual' consciousness in rather basic terms. By now you should have the general idea that we need to raise consciousness from the sacrum to the skull—from the root chakra to the crown chakra—and at the end of this "straightway path" we will have direct contact with God. Now the Bible goes much deeper into the journey. Exodus gets much more specific on exactly how this journey is to be taken.

As we move towards the specific instructions on opening your spiritual centers remember the *context* in which the Bible was compiled. We are in the Roman Empire. The punishment for worshipping anything other than the traditional Roman gods is imprisonment or death. The authors of the Old and New Testaments have learned how to attain enlightenment. They don't want to share the knowledge with the political class, or anyone unprepared to hear the message. So the writers hide their knowledge in parables and metaphors. The authors create stories that seem like they are about one thing when actually they are about something else. These stories are difficult to write. The author has to find a balance between getting the profound details correct but hidden in a story that seems like it is about something completely different. Often times there are levels of distortion to hide the truth. On one level the stories seem like mythology. One another level, as the Princeton University religious scholar Elaine Pagels has identified, the stories seem like they are political, or "wartime literature" about the evils of Rome. Neither of these types of stories—myth or history—is worthy of a sacredly profound book like the Bible. Hopefully, you understand by now we are talking about a much more universal and profound experience. We are talking about *your* journey to God. We are talking about the journey where the "Son of Man" becomes the "Son of God." There is *nothing* more important in this life than that!

So how do you hide such a divine story when your life is at stake? You use *symbolism* that is hard (but not impossible) to decipher. You use metaphor. You use one word, like "breastplate," to mean the chest, or more accurately the heart. The instructions for opening the pineal gland are not unique to Judaism and Christianity. Hinduism, and many more sacred texts, also describe the pineal gland meditation. So we can cross-reference across the religious spectrum for clarity on certain concepts.

So let's once again start at the very beginning of the spiritual journey to Christ Consciousness.

Exodus Chapter 23,
> *Thou shalt not raise a false report: put not thine hand with the wicked to be an unrighteous witness.*

Be righteous. Be a good person.

Exodus Chapter 23:10-11
> *And six years thou shalt sow thy land, and shalt gather*

> *in the fruits thereof: But the seventh year thou shalt let it rest and lie still*

Do the inner work on your lower chakras. Rise from lower consciousness to higher consciousness and "gather the fruits" (benefits of your work). The seventh chakra can only be activated with stillness (deep meditation).

Exodus Chapter 23:14-15
> *Three times thou shalt keep a feast unto me in the year. Thou shall keep the feast of unleavened bread: thou shalt eat unleavened bread seven days*

Bring body, mind, and soul into alignment while in meditation. Keep your mind free of thoughts (unleavened bread = thoughts that have not risen).

Exodus Chapter 23:16
> *And the feast of harvest, the firstfruits of thy labours, which thou hast sown in the field: and the feast of ingathering, which is in the end of the year, when thou hast gathered in thy labors out of the field.*

The "feast of harvest" is your efforts in meditation. Your working hard to overcome your incessant thoughts (materiality, the "field"). You labors (effort) will bring you out of the field (materiality).

Exodus Chapter 23:19
> *The first of the firstfruits of thy land thou shalt bring into the house of the LORD thy God, Thou shalt not*

> *seethe a kid in his mother's milk.*

The "firstfruits" is the benefit you receive from quieting your mind. "Thy land" is your consciousness (your energy centers under the influence of the spiritual glands). Bring your exalted state of being (free of incessant, negative thoughts) up to the house of the LORD (focus your quieted presence at your pineal gland). Your consciousness generating energy centers are operating at an optimal state. You have transformed your old consciousness (negative thinking) to new consciousness (quieted mind). Do "not seethe a kid in his mother's milk" means to be aware not to let your consciousness slip back to negative thoughts. Do not revert back to your previous consciousness. Your energy centers (consciousness) are now new ("kid"), don't let them go back to their old influences ("mother's milk").

> Exodus Chapter 23:20
> *Behold, I send an Angel before thee, to keep thee in the way, and to bring thee into the place which I have prepared.*

God will send an Angel to guide you through the resurrection (ascension) process. Quite literally you will know this presence is with you. You are NOT going through the regeneration process alone.

> Exodus Chapter 23:23
> *For mine Angel shall go before thee, and bring thee in unto the Am'-o-rites, and the Hit'-tites, and the Per'-iz'-zites, and the Ca'-na-an-ites, the Hi'-vites, and Jeb'-u-sites: and I will cut them off.*

The Angel will help you move your way up through the lower six energy centers. When you get to the top energy center (the pituitary gland) God will "cut off" the influence of lower consciousness in the lower six energy centers. You will have reached enlightenment. You are born again. You have attained Christ Consciousness.

Exodus Chapter 23:25
> *And ye shall serve the LORD your God, and he shall bless thy bread, and thy water; and I will take sickness away from the midst of thee.*

Your life will be blessed when you make it to spiritual consciousness. A major benefit of having Kundalini is that you become much less susceptible to illness. When your energy centers are wide open and operating efficiently healing energy is entering into your body keeping you healthier than is typical for most humans.

Exodus Chapter 23:27/29/30/33
> *I will send my fear before thee, and will destroy all the people to whom thou shalt come, and I will make all thine enemies turn their backs unto thee... I will not drive them out from before thee in one year; lest the land become desolate, and the beast of the field multiply against thee... By little and little I will drive them out from before thee, until thou be increased, and inherit the land... They (your enemies) shall not dwell in thy land, lest they make thee sin against me: for thou serve their gods, it will surely be a snare unto thee.*

Wow. We are really getting to the meat of what happens when your spiritual centers are activated here. The passage is saying that once your spiritual centers are open and you are at 'Spiritual' consciousness, you will have the willpower to turn away your "enemies" (negative thoughts, lower consciousness). This process will take time. Your energy centers are being "reset" to 'Spiritual' consciousness. The pineal gland meditation must be performed at least three separate times. This doesn't happen all at once because then you would have the conditions for a vacuum. Any thoughts you have in this vacuum could overrun any spiritual advancement you've made. Think of it like a blood transfusion. The transfusion happens over time. They don't take all your blood out and then give you new blood. It's a slow exchange until the old blood is out, leaving you with new, clean blood. The last part of the passage is a warning not to slip back into lower consciousness. Be AWARE of your thoughts during meditation. Don't let your thoughts sink back to lower consciousness. Don't let envy, low self-esteem, anger, etc… back into your awareness. Be vigilant about keeping your mind clear of negative thoughts. If you start thinking negatively you will fall into a trap and you will not maintain 'Spiritual' consciousness.

Exodus Chapter 24 is subtitled *Moses Meets God on the Mount*. This means Moses has succeeded in his meditation of quieting his mind. He has removed the negative thoughts that are associated with active lower consciousness. Moses is ready to meet God "on the mount" (he is ready to bring his focus onto the pineal gland).

Exodus Chapter 24:1,2
And he said unto Mo'-ses, Come up unto the LORD….

> *And Moses alone shall come near the LORD: but they shall not come nigh: neither shall the people go up with him.*

Moses is to "*come up*" to the LORD. LORD (God in Moses) is waiting for Moses at the pineal gland. When Moses activates the pineal gland in his deep meditation the literal doorway to God is opened. The "people" ('Human' consciousness) shall NOT go with him. Moses must stay in 'Spiritual' consciousness for the pineal gland to open.

> Exodus Chapter 24:4,5
> *And Mo'-ses wrote all the words of the LORD, and rose up early in the morning, and builded an alter under the hill... And he sent young men of the children of Is'-ra-el, which offered burnt offerings, and sanctified peace offerings of oxen unto the LORD.*

Moses "wrote all the words of the LORD, and rose up early in the morning," means Moses is in deep meditation and the state of his mind is 'Spiritual' consciousness. The "alter" Moses is building is the quieted presence he is giving the pineal gland. The "young men of the children of Israel" is the new spiritual conscious energy being generated by the body's energy centers. "The children of Israel" always means the body's energy centers under the influence of 'Spiritual' consciousness. So the pairing of "children of Israel" with "young men" means the new spiritual energy being generated by the body's energy centers. "Burnt offerings" is the active focusing of Kundalini energy onto the pineal gland. "Peace offering" is quiet meditation. "Sanctified" oxen means 'Animal' consciousness is being transformed to 'Spiritual' consciousness.

The passage is telling us that *the process of engaging your pineal gland is transforming normal consciousness into spiritual consciousness.* The pineal gland, "the command center for life," is making its influence felt on the lower five glands. This is the ascension process. Also known as resurrection or the second birth. This is the beginning of the "Son of Man" becoming the "Son of God." 'Animal' and 'Human' consciousness is being transformed into 'Spiritual' consciousness.

> Exodus Chapter 24:15-18
>
> *And Mo'-ses went up into the mount, and a cloud covered the mount. And the glory of the LORD abode upon mount Si'-nai, and the cloud covered it six days: and the seventh day he called unto Mo'-ses out of the midst of the cloud. And the sight of the glory of the LORD was like devouring fire on top of the mount in the eyes of the children of Is'-ra-el. And Mo'-ses went into the midst of the cloud, and gat him up into the mount: and Mo'-ses was in the mount for forty days and forty nights.*

There is so much literal and figurative symbolism happening in this passage. This is the peak meditation experience. This is the moment you meet LORD (God in you). Moses has directed Kundalini energy and his presence at his pineal gland. You will notice from here on out that the term *cloud* is heavily used in the Bible. When you open your pineal gland you will be enveloped with clouds; both in your mind's eye and in your physical space. Moses is called out of the clouds on the seventh day. He has engaged all seven of his energy centers. The "devouring fire" is characterizing the sight of the LORD that you will experience in your mind's eye. Yogananda explains "Just behind the darkness of closed eyes in meditation shines the radiance of God."[44] Meeting God in meditation is an earth-shattering event and impossible to describe with words. The descriptions in the Bible are approximations of what you will experience first hand. The number forty indicates the completion of the ascension process. Moses has successfully raised his consciousness to 'Spiritual' consciousness.

Exodus Chapter 25 moves deeper into what will happen to you during the pineal gland activation. The chapter is subtitled *Instructions for a Tabernacle* which is actually instructions for the pineal gland. There is no physical tabernacle. This is the meaning of the passage in Acts 7:48 "Temples not made of hands." We are not talking about real temples. This is a temple made by God. Between your temples is the location of the pineal gland.

There is a lot of symbolism and metaphor in Chapter 25. Remember all of this is happening in deep meditation. To get to this point in meditation you must have Kundalini energy (Moses' rod that turns into a serpent) and a quieted mind. This is the meditation that opens the pineal gland. The meditation is very complex and so it will be described over and over again for the rest of the chapters in Exodus and at the beginning of Leviticus.

> Exodus Chapter 25:1-2
> *And the LORD spake unto Mo'-ses, saying, Speak unto the children of Is'-ra-el, that they bring me an offering: of every man that giveth it willingly with his heart ye shall take my offering.*

The term spake shows we are talking about energy. In 'Spiritual' consciousness (no negative thoughts) bring an "offering" (go into meditation). Do this with a willing, open heart. An open heart chakra is critical to opening the pineal gland chakra.

This is a meeting between you and God. Bring your "offering" (a quieted mind) and God will give you an "offering" (resurrection, the "second birth").

> Exodus Chapter 25:3-8
> *And this is the offering which he shall take of them; gold, and silver, and brass. And blue, and purple, and scarlet, and fine linen, and goat's hair. And rams' skins dyed red, and badgers' skins, and shit'-tim wood, Oil for the light, spices for anointing oil, and sweet incense. Onyx stones, and stones to be set in the e'-phod, and in the breastplate. And let them make me a sanctuary; that I may dwell among them.*

These are the symbolic elements of the "tabernacle." This would be a ridiculous tabernacle if taken literally. These are not literal descriptions of a physical place. These are metaphorical descriptions of the pineal gland meditation. When you are meditating on the pineal gland you will see in your mind's eye very specific imagery. You are connecting with another dimension. You are opening your "third eye." Your connection to the spirit world is clearer once the pineal gland is open.

All of the terms in the above passages are describing the pineal gland meditation. The metals are most likely describing the trinity of The Father, the Son, and the Holy Ghost—God being gold and man being brass. The colors are the energy centers. You will see multicolored light particles in your mind's eye. Shit'-tim wood we will talk about in the next passage. "Oil for the light" is presence on your energy centers. Presence is what makes the energy centers expand thereby increasing conscious energy within your body. "Sweet incense" is quiet presence (no thoughts). An ephod is similar to a coat. The terms ephod and coat throughout the Bible are interchangeable. They both refer to the seven chakras. "Breastplate" is a focus on the heart chakra. The key to opening the spiritual centers is the heart chakra. The key to God is love.

> Exodus Chapter 25:10
> *And they shall make an ark of shit'-tim wood: two cubits and a half shall be the length therof, and a cubit and a half the breadth therof, and a cubit and a half the height therof.*

This is a very interesting passage. *Shit'-tim* is an unusual name. And notice the word *half* is repeated three times. Whenever a word is repeated in the Bible it requires attention. So here we have the unusual term shit'-tim followed by an emphasis on the term half. The instruction here is to halve the word shit'-tim. What we end up with is the sound "sha," which points to the mantra sound Sham. The mantra Sham is one of the most important factors of opening your pineal gland. The vibrational frequency you create by saying the word Sham corresponds to the pineal gland. The vibrations set the stage for engaging the pineal gland energy center. When you are in the pineal gland meditation repeat the word Sham. Don't try to intellectualize this instruction. When you have Kundalini and you are ready to engage your pineal gland this will all make sense. You will feel the difference in your energy level when you start to chant the mantra Sham.

> Exodus Chapter 25:17-22
> *And thou shalt make a mercy seat of pure gold… And thou shalt make two cher'-u-bims of gold… in the two ends of the mercy seat… And make one cher'-u-bim on*

> *the one end, and the other cher'-ub on the other end: even of the mercy seat shall ye make the cher'-u-bims on the two ends therof. And the cher'-u-bims shall stretch forth their wings on high covering the mercy seat with their wings, and their faces shall look one to another; toward the mercy seat shall the faces of the cher'-u-bims be. And there I will meet with thee, and I will commune with thee from above the mercy seat, from between the two cher'-u-bims...*

This is a very poetic passage. These are instructions on where you are to place your focus during your meditation in order to commune with the LORD. As we discussed earlier in this book, the cherubims are metaphors for the two halves of the brain. The mercy seat is the pineal gland that is located between the two halves of the brain.

Exodus Chapter 28 goes into a very detailed breathing technique.

> *And thou shalt make upon the breastplate chains at the ends of the wreathen work. And thou shalt make upon the breastplate two rings of gold and shalt put the two rings on the two ends of the breastplate... And the other two ends of the two wreathen chains thou shalt fasten in the two ouches, and put them on the shoulder-pieces of the ephod before it.*

The term *breastplate* tells us one location of the breath work ("wreathen work") is to be located in the chest or heart. We must breath into the heart space in our chest. When we sketch out the sets of rings on a piece of paper we notice that the two rings form an infinity (or figure 8) sign. This is a type of breathing that circulates breath, and energy, throughout your body from the sacrum to the skull. The "connection" point of the two "rings" is at your throat ("shoulder pieces"). In Hinduism this breathing technique is part of Kriya yoga. A full explanation of this breathing technique can be found in the book *Kundalini Tantra* by Satyananda Saraswati.

> Exodus Chapter 28:29
> *And Aa'-ron shall bear the names of the children of Is'-ra-el in the breastplate of judgment in his heart, when he goeth in unto the holy place, for a memorial before the LORD continually.*

After using the infinity breathing technique that circulates breath and divine energy to all of the chakras, Aaron must also have an open heart center as he sets his presence on the pineal gland to meet with the LORD.

> Exodus Chapter 28:36-38
> *And thou shalt make a plate of pure gold, and grave upon it, like the engraving of a signet, HOLINESS TO THE LORD. And thou shalt put it on a blue lace, that it may be upon the mitre; upon the forefront of the mitre it shall be. And it shall be upon Aa'-ron's forehead, ... and it shall be always upon his forehead, that they may be accepted before the LORD.*

So from the previous passage we are doing deep circulating infinity breathing. This is increasing the speed of Kundalini and bringing divine energy throughout our body. Next we have a prayer HOLINESS TO THE LORD. We are about to meet the LORD (God in us). The "blue lace" is telling us where our focus is to be at this point. Blue is the color associated with the throat energy center. A *mitre* is a guide. At this point in the meditation we are trying to direct Kundalini energy at the pineal gland. This is a very difficult task. We have laser thin Kundalini flowing very quickly trying to hit the very small pineal gland in the middle of our brain. We need a mitre, or a guide, to direct the energy flow to the correct location. The "mitre" is the tongue. The tongue is to be placed on the roof of the mouth so that as Kundalini energy passes through the mouth it follows the path of the tongue and is directed to the middle of the brain. The term *forehead* is repeated twice. During this meditation your eyes should gaze to the forehead. This also helps focus and guide the energy to the pineal gland.

At this point in Exodus we are introduced to several repeated terms like *consecrate, bullock,* and *ram.* Consecrate means to concentrate (and literally means to *make sacred*). Bullock means to engage your buttock muscles (this helps "pull" up the energy from the sacrum/root chakra). Ram is describing forceful breath. The point of this meditation is to pierce the pineal gland with extremely fast moving energy. To increase the flow of Kundalini you will need to do heavy diaphragmatic breathing. When ram is mentioned you need to propel the energy up into the pineal gland with your breath.

In Exodus Chapter 29, the pineal gland meditation is described with Aaron. In Chapters 30 and 31 the meditation is described again with Moses (this time with a focus on the pituitary gland). The techniques are very complex and may seem quite odd for someone not familiar with meditating. You need to focus on several techniques at the same time. There are different breathing techniques that do different things with the energy in your body. Additionally, you must focus your attention on different locations of your body concurrently. This meditation can take many days to figure out correctly. The significant portion of Chapter 29 is listed here,

> *And this is the thing that thou shalt do... take one young bullock, and two rams without blemish, And unleavened bread, and cakes unleavened tempered with oil, and wafers unleavened anointed with oil... And thou shalt put them in one basket... And Aa'-ron and his sons thou shalt bring unto the door of the tabernacle of the congregation and shalt wash them with water. And thou shalt take the garments and put upon Aa'-ron the coat... And thou shalt put the mitre upon his head, and put the holy crown upon the mitre. Then thou shalt take the anointing oil and pour it upon his head... and the priest's office shall be theirs for a perpetual statue: and thou shalt consecrate Aa'-ron and his sons. And thou shalt cause a bullock to be brought before the tabernacle... and thou shalt kill the bullock before the LORD, by the door of the tabernacle. And thou shalt take all the fat that covert the inwards, and the caul that is above the kidneys, and the fat that is upon them, and burn them upon the alter... Thou shalt take one ram... and thou shalt slay the ram... about upon the alter. And thou shalt cut the ram in pieces and wash the inwards of him, and his legs, and put them into his pieces, and into his head. And thou shalt burn the whole ram upon the alter: it is a burnt offering unto the LORD: it is a sweet savour, an offering made by fire to the LORD... And thou shalt take*

the other ram... then shalt kill the ram... and put it on the right ear of Aa'-ron... the right ear of the sons, and upon the thumb or the right hand, upon the toe of the right foot... Also thou shalt take of the ram the fat and the rump.... For it is a ram of consecration. And thou shalt put all in the hands of Aa'-ron, and in the hands of his sons; and shalt wave them for a wave offering before the LORD. And thou shalt receive them of their hands, and burn them upon the alter for a burnt offering, for a sweet savour before the LORD: It is an offering made by fire unto the LORD. And thou shalt take the breast of the ram of Aaron's consecration and wave it for a wave offering before the LORD: and it shall be thy part. And thou shalt sanctify the breast of the wave offering, and the shoulder of the heave offering, which is waved, and which is heaved up, of the ram of the consecration, even of that which is for Aa'-ron... And it shall be Aa'-ron's and his sons by a statute for ever... for it is an heave offering: and it shall be a heave offering from the children of Is'-ra-el of the sacrifice of their peace offerings, even the heave offering unto the LORD. And that son that is priest in his stead put them on seven days, when he cometh into the tabernacle... And thou shalt take the ram of the consecration, and seethe his flesh in the holy place. And they shall eat those things wherewith the atonement was made and to sanctify them: but a stranger shall not eat thereof, because they are holy. Seven days thou shalt make an atonement for the altar, and sanctify it: and it shall be an altar most holy: whatsoever toucheth the altar shall be holy. Now this is that which thou shalt

> *offer upon the alter; two lambs of the first year day by day continually. The one lamb thou shalt offer in the morning; and the other thou shalt offer in the even:... This shall be a continual burnt offering throughout your generations at the door of the tabernacle of the congregation before the LORD: where I will meet you... And I will dwell among the children of Is'-ra-el, and I will be their God. And they shall know that I am their God, that I brought them forth out of the land of E'-gypt, that I may dwell among them: I am the LORD their God.*

Whew. That is a lot of information. The meditation to meet God is no joke. It is very complex. Let's take another look at Chapter 29 with the metaphors explained.

> *And this is the thing that thou shalt do... take one young bullock, and two rams without blemish, And unleavened bread, and cakes unleavened tempered with oil, and wafers unleavened anointed with oil... And thou shalt put them in one basket...*

These are the tools of the meditation: bullock means to contract the buttocks, ram is breathing with force, unleavened means to have a quieted mind (no thoughts are rising).

> *And Aa'-ron and his sons thou shalt bring unto the door of the tabernacle of the congregation and shalt wash them with water.*

Aaron and his sons are the body's energy centers. This passage is saying to prepare your energy centers for the transformation from lower consciousness to spiritual consciousness. The tabernacle is the pineal gland. We are beginning the process of bringing the lower energy centers under the influence of the spiritual centers. Wash means to breath. We are going to use the "infinity" breathing technique to cycle energy throughout the body bringing refined divine energy to each of the chakras.

> *And thou shalt take the garments and put upon Aa'-ron the coat...*

Bring your focus on all seven of the energy centers.

> *And thou shalt put the mitre upon his head, and put the holy crown upon the mitre.*

Place your tongue (the mitre) on the roof of your mouth (head). Kundalini energy is flowing up your spine and into your throat. The "holy crown" energy will follow the path of your tongue, which is pointing to the center of your brain which is where the pineal gland is located.

> *Then thou shalt take the anointing oil and pour it upon his head... and the priest's office shall be theirs for a perpetual statue: and thou shalt consecrate Aa'-ron and his sons.*

The "anointing oil" is the oxygenated mixture of air and energy. The oil is going to "light" the lamps (chakras). The term "priest" refers to someone who has opened their pineal gland. Perpetual means "occurring repeatedly," This is a long meditation.

Continue breathing. Consecrate Aaron and his sons means to concentrate on the energy centers. You are making Aaron and his sons (the energy centers) sacred by replacing human consciousness (energy) with spiritual consciousness (divine energy.)

> *And thou shalt cause a bullock to be brought before the tabernacle... and thou shalt kill the bullock before the LORD, by the door of the tabernacle.*

Contract your buttock muscles to thrust the energy from the root chakra to the pineal gland. You will feel the energy rise up to your pineal gland, with heightened concentration you are to stop the energy at the pineal gland.

> *And thou shalt take all the fat that covert the inwards, and the caul that is above the kidneys, and the fat that is upon them, and burn them upon the alter...*

You will feel the energy pass through your body, as it passes your kidneys you will hear and feel the energy burning your fat deposits. The fat is being used as fuel for the enhanced energy.

> *Thou shalt take one ram... and thou shalt slay the ram... about upon the alter*

Use deep forceful breath to pierce the pineal gland with Kundalini.

> *And thou shalt cut the ram in pieces and wash the inwards of him, and his legs, and put them into his pieces, and into his head. And thou shalt burn the whole ram upon the alter*

Cutting the ram means to diffuse your breath. Legs and head indicate full body breathing. Circulate your breath throughout your body. When your body is full of oxygenated energy focus the energy onto the alter (pineal gland) and use forceful breathing to ram (pierce) the pineal gland. Your body will be very warm at this point as you continue your heavy breathing. Kundalini is speeding up.

> *it is a burnt offering unto the LORD: it is a sweet savour, an offering made by fire to the LORD*

A burnt offering is Kundalini energy being heated up. You are in the process of enlightenment. You are literally burning up your negative thoughts and karma. Your negative thoughts are being transformed into peace of mind. You are moving towards lasting peace, God's goal for humanity. Burning negative thoughts is the sweet savor for the Lord. Burning an actual animal is not a sweet smell to the Lord! This is radical soul transformation.

> *And thou shalt take the other ram... then shalt kill the ram... and put it on the right ear of Aa'-ron... the right ear of the sons, and upon the thumb or the right hand, upon the toe of the right foot...*

Focus on the right side of your body. Energy is entering your body through your right foot and right hand.

> *Also thou shalt take of the ram the fat and the rump....*
> *For it is a ram of consecration*

Continue to concentrate. Remember you may be doing this meditation for hours, if not days, until you get the hang of it. You will need to maintain concentration for extended periods of time.

> *And thou shalt put all in the hands of Aa'-ron, and in the hands of his sons; and shalt wave them for a wave offering before the LORD*

Wave means to breath in waves. You're pulling the energy from the sacrum to the skull in waves of breath.

> *And thou shalt receive them of their hands, and burn them upon the alter for a burnt offering, for a sweet savour before the lord*

"Burn" your thoughts.

> *It is an offering made by fire unto the LORD*

Kundalini is the chariot for this meditation. It is heated Kundalini energy that pierces the pineal gland.

> *And thou shalt take the breast of the ram of Aaron's consecration and wave it for a wave offering before the LORD: and it shall be thy part. And thou shalt sanctify the breast of the wave offering, and the shoulder of the heave offering, which is waved, and which is heaved up, of the ram of the consecration*

Breath forcefully. Concentrate. Pull the energy up your spine to the throat and then heave it into your skull. This process has a steep learning curve. These instructions will likely not make sense to the casual reader who is not actively engaged in the experience. For someone who hasn't experienced the sensation of energy flowing through their body, it may be impossible to comprehend the specifics of this meditation that engages your pineal gland. When you actually have Kundalini energy running up your spine it isn't such an intellectual leap to understand the instructions. Initially, it may take some time to fulfill the requirements of this meditation. But after you do it once the second and third time will be much quicker and easier. Yes, this meditation needs to be performed at least three times.

> *even of that which is for Aa'-ron... And it shall be Aa'-ron's and his sons by a statute for ever... for it is an heave offering: and it shall be a heave offering from the children of Is'-ra-el of the sacrifice of their peace offerings, even the heave offering unto the LORD. And that son that is priest in his stead put them on seven days, when he cometh into the tabernacle*

Continue to heave. You are in the process of transforming the energy of lower consciousness into the energy of higher consciousness. Maintain a meditative state of mind. Focus on your seven chakras, clear your mind of thoughts, heave the energy with wave breath into your pineal gland.

> *And thou shalt take the ram of the consecration, and seethe his flesh in the holy place*

With powerful breath "burn" (propel) the heated energy into your pineal gland (holy place).

And they shall eat those things wherewith the atonement was made and to sanctify them:

Be at one with the LORD. Be still.

but a stranger shall not eat thereof, because they are holy. Seven days thou shalt make an atonement for the altar, and sanctify it: and it shall be an altar most holy: whatsoever toucheth the altar shall be holy. Now this is that which thou shalt offer upon the alter; two lambs of the first year day by day continually. The one lamb thou shalt offer in the morning; and the other thou shalt offer in the even... This shall be a continual burnt offering throughout your generations

If the meditation is not successful you are deemed a "stranger." If you become a stranger keep meditating until you are successful. For the rest of your life you are to meditate each morning and each night. Kundalini will always be with you.

at the door of the tabernacle of the congregation before the LORD: where I will meet you... And I will dwell among the children of Is'-ra-el, and I will be their God. And they shall know that I am their God

God will appear to you, and you will know it without doubt. If God doesn't appear the meditation was not successful.

that I brought them forth out of the land of E'-gypt, that I may dwell among them: I am the LORD their God.

Your energy centers have been "reset" with divine energy. You are at the initial stages of 'Spiritual' consciousness.

At this point in Exodus Chapter 30 the instructions are repeated for Moses. Each time the meditation is repeated there are added instructions. The repetition helps the initiate to remember the instructions.

> *And the LORD spake unto Mo'-ses, saying... This they shall give, every one that passeth among them that are numbered, half a she'-kel after the she'-kel of the sanctuary: (a she'-kel is twenty ge'-rahs:) an half she'-kel shall be the offering to the LORD.*

This is a strange passage. It seems highly unusual to have to put an explanation in parenthesis that "a she'-kel is twenty ge'-rahs." Why distinguish a value for something that must fluctuate with time? It would be like taking note of today's exchange rate and then memorializing it in profound sacred scripture. It wouldn't make sense. It's an insignificant detail in the scheme of things. This is another writing technique to inform the reader that there is more to the passage than meets the eye. The important thing to take notice of in this passage is the repetition of the words she'-kel and half. This instruction is exactly the same as the earlier passages about shit'-tim wood. We are to halve the word she'-kel to get the sound "sha" which points to the mantra Sham. The biblical passage is an instruction to repeatedly say the mantra Sham. In this meditation you want to begin by repeatedly chanting out loud, or under your breath, the mantra Sham. You will notice a marked difference in the resonance of your energy as you begin to say or whisper the word Sham. You must be in deep meditation and have a strong Kundalini flow to realize this effect.

> *Everyone that passeth among them that are numbered from twenty years old and above, shall give an offering unto the LORD.*

Repeat the Sham mantra at least twenty times.

> *And thou shalt take the atonement money of the children of Is'-ra-el and shalt appoint it for the service of the tabernacle*

Be at one with the LORD. Be still. Maintain spiritual consciousness as you bring your awareness to the pineal gland.

> *When they go into the tabernacle, they shall wash with water, that they die; or when they come near to the alter to minister, to burn offering made by fire unto the LORD*

Wash with water means to cleanse your body with breath. Keep the heavy breathing going at all times or the meditation will end. The burnt offering is meditation with heated Kundalini.

> *Moreover the LORD spake to Mo'-ses saying, take thou also unto thee principal spices, of pure myrrh five hundred she'-kels, and of sweet cinnamon half so much, even two hundred and fifty she'-kels, and of sweet calamus two hundred and fifty she'-kels.*

The repetition of the word she'-kels points to the mantra Sham. Myrrh is an antiseptic. In traditional Chinese medicine myrrh is used to increase the circulation of blood. Blood is life. The Holy Spirit flows through the right hand in the blood stream. Cinnamon is a warming spice. It represents the heat that will be, or needs to be, generated within the body during meditation. Cinnamon can be ingested to balance out the body's temperature. Calamus is a word derived from reed, straw, or cane. It's symbolic of the spine. In Greek mythology calamus is also symbolic of love. Having an open and willing heart is crucial to a meditation practice. The passage is describing some of the key elements of the meditation and continues in the next passage:

> *And the LORD said unto Mo'-ses, Take unto thee sweet spices, stac'-te, and on'-y-cha, and gal'-ba-num; these sweet spices with pure frankincense: of each shall there be like a weight:*

The ingredients of the "incense" are metaphorically pointing to the elements of the meditation: Stacte is a viscous liquid, thick but not solid, similar to *sap*. Onycha was a balm used to remove impurities.[45] The Hebrew meaning of the word has been translated as "a peeling off by concussion of *sound*,"[46] and has been compared to the roar of a lion. The galbanum plant has long hollow stems. The Latin name for galbanum is *ferula* which refers to a *rod*. So the elements of the meditation are the sap that is Kundalini energy which has the consistency of being denser than air but lighter than water (thick but not solid). Sound vibration pulsating along the spine refers to *mantra*. It is the vibratory effect of repeating the word Sham that sets the stage for opening the pineal gland. Rod refers to the hollow spinal column where Kundalini flows from the sacrum into the skull. In traditional Chinese medicine frankincense is used to move qi (vital energy).

Energy is moved by *presence* so frankincense is symbolic of a quieted mind in meditation. So the elements of the meditation are Kundalini, mantra, spinal activity, and presence.

> *And thou shalt make it a perfume, a confection after the art of apothecary, tempered together, pure and holy*

Assemble all of the ingredients of the meditation: Kundalini, mantra, spinal activity, and presence. The combination is holy, of God.

> *And thou shalt beat some of it very small, and put it before the testimony in the tabernacle of the congregation, where I will meet with thee: it shall be unto you most holy*

During this meditation you will be juggling a lot of balls. There are many aspects to this meditation. You will be breathing heavily for an extended period of time and the energy you create inside of your body will be tremendous. When you are ready to pierce the gland you will need to focus the energy into one small physical location at the pineal gland in the center of your skull. This is a refined meditation. Once you engage the pineal gland LORD will appear.

> *And as for the perfume which thou shalt make, ye shall not make to yourself according to the composition thereof: it shall be unto thee holy for the LORD*

The meditation needs to be precise. All of the elements need to be present for the meditation to be successful. Which means the pineal gland is engaged for a prolonged amount of time, then the pineal gland will expand as the heated Kundalini energy "charges" the gland. The expanded pineal gland will release refined 'Spiritual' consciousness into your skull.

In Exodus Chapter 31 the instructions focus on engaging the pituitary gland. The energy centers associated with the pineal and pituitary glands are intimately connected. The pineal gland energy center is said to be the gateway to the pituitary gland center. The process of ascension to this point has been a "fading of normal consciousness and a development of higher awareness."[47] As Kundalini rises to the pineal gland lower consciousness is being replaced by higher consciousness. Transcendence begins. When Kundalini reaches the pituitary gland energy center enlightenment begins to unfold.

> *And the LORD spake unto Mo'-ses saying, See I have called by name the Be-zal'-e-el the son of U'-ri, the son of Hur, of the tribe of Ju'-dah: And I have filled him with the spirit of God, in wisdom, and understanding, and in knowledge and in all manner of workmanship*

Bezaleel is the "chief artisan" of the tabernacle (the pituitary gland). The pituitary gland is the doorway to enlightenment, knowledge, and wisdom. Your dormant brain centers are being activated. You will become a master or genius of your vocation. Swami Satyananda Saraswati explains that people who manage to awaken all of their energy centers with Kundalini (or are already born in this state) become "superior people in every aspect of life. They are the great thinkers, musicians, artists, builders, scientists, research scholars, inventors, prophets, statesmen, and so on."[48]

> *Six days may work be done; but in the seventh is the sabbath of rest, holy to the LORD: whosoever doeth any work in the sabbath day, he shall surely be put to death*

Recall from earlier in this book that the esoteric meaning of the ten commandments are about meditation. When you are raising consciousness to the Spirit level you must work on your lower chakras. When you are engaging the upper spiritual centers, particularly the seventh chakra, the pituitary gland, you must be present in silence. You must have a quieted mind free from negative, incessant thoughts. If you try and engage the pituitary gland with an active mind you will be put to "death," meaning the meditation session will be over. You will not be reborn. You will not go from being the Son of Man to the Son of God. You will stay at lower consciousness until you get the meditation done correctly.

> *And he (LORD) gave unto Mo'-ses, when he had made an end of communing with him upon mount Si'-nai, two tables of testimony, written with the finger of God*

When you have engaged both the pineal and pituitary glands your commune with God is complete.

Exodus Chapter 32
> *And when the people saw that Mo'-ses delayed to come down out of the mount, the people gathered themselves together unto Aa'-ron, and said unto him, Up, make us gods, which shall go before us; for as for this Mo'-ses, the man that brought us up out of the land of E'-gypt, we wot not what is become of him.*

This is an important passage. It is telling us a lot about what it means to engage your pituitary gland. Accessing the pineal gland is a relatively quick meditation. You can probably complete it in seven days. The pituitary gland takes much more time to fully awaken. So in this passage the "people" are waiting for Moses to come out of his deep meditation. The "people" are symbolic of 'Human' consciousness. So first we have Moses being "delayed from coming down from the mount." This tells us the pituitary meditation will take a long time—months, years, or a lifetime. Then we have the term "Up" which is a hint that our focus needs to go to the top of the skull; the location of the pituitary gland energy center (not the physical location of the gland). Then we have "make us gods." Engaging the pituitary gland is the realization of 'Spiritual' consciousness. Otherwise known as Christ Consciousness. The Son of Man becomes the Son of God.

At this juncture in Exodus we get to arguably the most incredible part of the entire Bible. We are at Chapter 32 of Exodus. In Chapter 32 of Genesis we had Jacob rising to a place, *"And Jacob called the name of the place Pe-ni'-el: for I have seen God face to face, and my life is preserved."* Jacob makes it to the pineal gland and he sees God. Now, we are at the next Chapter 32 in the Old Testament, and the author's of Exodus begin to describe the visual experience you will have when you meet God.

> Exodus Chapter 32:2-3
> *And Aa'-ron said unto them, Break off the golden earrings, which are in the ears of your wives, of your sons, and of your daughters, and bring them unto me. And all the people brake off the golden earrings which were in their ears, and brought them to Aa'-ron.*

The emphasis here is on the words *ear, gold,* and *rings.* Ear is the location of the action. The visualizations happen between your ears in your mind's eye. When you are in this deep meditation you will see gold colored rings. In Hinduism, this golden ring of light in the spiritual eye is "the microcosmic objective cosmic energy, Cosmic Vibration, or Holy Ghost."[49]

Exodus Chapter 32:4-5
> *And he received them at their hand, and fashioned it with a graving tool, after he had made it a golden calf: and they said These be thy gods, O Is'-ra-el, which brought thee up out of the land of E'-gypt.*

In meditation you will see a golden "calf" (a shape that visually represents a calf). The "people" (lower consciousness) mistakenly think this vision must be God when they say "These be thy gods."

Exodus Chapter 32:7
> *And the LORD said unto Mo'-ses, Go, get thee down; for thy people, which thou broughtest out of the land of E'-gypt have corrupted themselves.*

"Go, get thee down," means to go back down into lower consciousness. The lower energy centers you've raised to 'Spiritual' consciousness have been corrupted by lower consciousness.

Exodus Chapter 32:8
> *They have turned aside quickly out of the way which I commanded them: they have made them a molten calf and have worshipped it, and have sacrificed thereunto,*

> *and said, These be thy god, O Is'-ra-el, which have brought thee up out of the land of E'-gypt.*

The lower energy centers have regressed from 'Spiritual' consciousness to lower consciousness. Meaning your mind has returned to incessant and negative thinking—the opposite direction of enlightenment. What this means in practical terms is that in your meditation you are seeing several visions. Among them you will see a golden "calf" shape. Don't get distracted by the shapes. The shapes are captivating and intriguing, but don't get fixated on them. Otherwise you will lose your mental focus. Move your awareness beyond these images.

> Exodus Chapter 32:9-10
> *And the LORD said unto Mo'-ses, I have seen this people, and, behold it is a stiffnecked people. Now therefore let me alone, that my wrath may wax hot against them, and that I may consume them: and I will make of thee a great nation.*

The first term to pay attention to is *stiffnecked*. It is an unusual term that is repeated often in the Bible. The message here is to keep your head perfectly still while you're in this deep meditation. Heated Kundalini is flowing through your neck into your skull. If you move the energy may lose its target of hitting the gland. You must maintain the path of the energetic flow. The heat being generated by deep diaphragmatic breathing and enhanced Kundalini will eventually "melt" away the images of the "calf."

> Exodus Chapter 32:15
> *And Mo'-ses turned, and went down from the mount,*

and the two tables of the testimony were in his hand...
And the tables were the work of God,

Moses turns back to the lower energy centers to bring them back under the influence of the two spiritual energy centers: the pineal and pituitary glands (the two tables); God's glands for divinity and enlightenment.

Exodus Chapter 32:17-18
And when Josh'-u-a heard the noise of the people as they shouted, he said unto Mo'-ses, There is a noise of war in the camp. And he said, it is not the voice of them that shout for mastery, neither is it the voice of them that cry for being overcome: but the noise of them that sing do I hear.

When 'Human' conscious is finally wrestled free of the impulses of lower consciousness, meaning when lower consciousness transforms into 'Spiritual' consciousness, it is a glorious thing for mankind. Practically speaking, when this transformation happens in meditation a loud hissing sound will be heard as divine energy is being released into your body. You have expanded the pineal gland with heated Kundalini energy. The expanded gland is now releasing divine energy into your body "resetting" your lower chakras.

Exodus Chapter 32:26-27
Then Mo'-ses stood in the gate of the camp, and said, Who is on the LORD's side? Let him come unto me... And he said unto them, Thus saith the LORD God of Is'-ra-el, Put every man his sword by his side, and go

> *in and out from gate to gate throughout the camp, and slay every man his brother, and every man his companion, and every man his neighbor.*

Oh how this passage has been misunderstood. How much killing did this passage justify in the times of the Christian crusades? This passage, like most of the passages in the Bible, are NOT meant to be taken literally. No on is being killed in the Bible. This is a metaphorical passage. The word "gate" always refers to the energy centers. We are at the point in the meditation where we are right at the "door" of the spiritual centers. We are about to leave 'Human' consciousness. The "man" that is being slayed is *human consciousness*. We are about to become spiritually enlightened. The "man," our *ego*, is about to be "slayed."

Exodus Chapter 32:34
> *Therefore now go, lead the people unto the place of which I have spoken unto thee: behold mine Angel shall go before thee: nevertheless in the day that I visit I will visit their sin upon them.*

'Human' consciousness is being raised to 'Spiritual' consciousness. The "people" are going up to the spiritual centers. In the meditation you have no thoughts, your mind is clear. The nagging, persistent thoughts that normally arise have subsided. In your visualizations you will see an Angel fly by in front of you. You are very close to seeing God.

Exodus Chapter 33
> *And the LORD said unto Mo'-ses, Depart, and go up hence, thou and the people which thou hast brought up*

*out of the land of E'-gypt, unto the land which I sware
unto A'-bra-ham, to I'-saac, and to Ja'-cob, saying Unto
thy seed will I give.*

God is summoning Moses to 'Spiritual' consciousness. The names listed are all decedents of Shem, symbolic of the pineal gland.

Exodus Chapter 33:2
*And I will send an angel before thee; and I will drive
out the Ca'-na-an-ite, the Am'-o-rite, and the Hit'-tite,
and the Per-iz'-zite, the Hi'-vite, and the Jeb'-u-site:*

An angel is overseeing this radical soul transformation. We are rising above the six lower chakras.

Exodus Chapter 32:3-7
*Unto a land flowing with milk and honey... For the
LORD had said unto Mo'-ses, Say unto the children
of Is'-ra-el, Ye are a stiffnecked people: I will come up
into the midst of thee in a moment, and consume thee;
therefore now put off thy ornaments from thee that I
may know what to do unto thee.*

God is about to "consume" human consciousness. To bring you into 'Spiritual' consciousness where life is nourishing and sweet (milk and honey). God will do this by literally passing over you and enveloping your body in divine energy. Remove any metal jewelry you may be wearing at this time. You must remain perfectly still while God passes over you. Be stiffnecked!

Exodus Chapter 33:9

And it came to pass, as Mo'-ses entered into the tabernacle, the cloudy pillar descended, and stood at the door of the tabernacle, and the LORD talked with Mo'-ses.

While in deep meditation, in your mind's eye, while focusing on the pineal gland, you will literally see a round disc descend onto you from the clouds. You will see clouds. Literally. The "cloudy pillar" is this disc that is approaching your pineal gland. You will hear God after the disc envelopes your mind's eye.

Exodus Chapter 33:11

And all the people saw the cloudy pillar stand at the tabernacle door: And all the people rose up and worshipped, every man in his tent door. And the LORD spake unto Mo'-se face to face, as a man speaketh unto his friend. And he turned again into the camp

You will see the cloudy pillar. "Every man at his tent door," means every energy center. Each of the chakras will feel the influence of meeting God. LORD (God in Moses) "spakes" (sparks... this is an energetic connection) to Moses face to face. Just like God spoke to Jacob face to face in Genesis Chapter 32.

Exodus Chapter 33:20

And he said, Thou canst not see my face: for there shall no man see me, and live.

This passage is completely misunderstood by almost everyone who reads it. The passage is not saying that it is impossible to see God and live. It is saying that no "man" will see God and live.

That means that you are no longer a man once you see God. You are not living in 'Human' consciousness anymore, you are living in 'Spiritual' consciousness. You are no longer the Son of Man, but the Son of God. You are as some mystics say a "junior god." Or as Jesus said in John 10:34 "Ye are gods." You are Christ Consciousness. This is the "second birth."

This same idea comes up again in John 1:18 "No man hath seen God at any time." For a comparison with Hindu thought I will insert here some commentary from Paramahansa Yogananda from his seminal work entitled *The Second Coming of Christ: The Resurrection of Christ Within You.* "If God is imperceptible, He must also be unknowable. How frustrating would seem one's efforts in meditation, or in prayer to such a reclusive God.... The word 'seen' has such a provisory connotation. One who is body bound, whose consciousness is limited to sensory perceptions... When man has lifted his consciousness from the ordinary sensory state to receive that only begotten Christ Consciousness, he also shall see God, not with mortal sight but with divine perception."[50] This is one area where the author of this book respectively disagrees with the yoga master. God is visible to the "initiate" in deep meditation with both the physical eyes and the single spiritual eye. The white stillness aspect of God appears to the physical eyes in the form of a cloud (also referred to as a mist in the Bible). The supersonic, multicolored aspect of God (differentiated in the Bible as LORD) appears in the spiritual eye.

> Exodus Chapter 33:21-23
>
> *And the LORD said, Behold there is a place by me, and thou shalt stand upon a rock: And it shall come to pass, while my glory passeth by, that I will put thee in a clift of the rock, and will cover thee with my hand while*

> *I pass by: And I will take away mine hand, and thou shalt see my back parts: but my face shall not be seen.*

The "rock" is the human brain. The "clift in the rock" is the seam that runs between the two halves of the brain. This is where the pineal gland is located. At this point in the meditation you are completely enveloped with brilliantly lit multicolored light particles flowing through your body into the pineal gland at sonic speeds. As this light approaches your pineal gland, the intensity of the movement forces your eyelids to constrict causing a temporary "black out" in your mind's eye. When your inner vision returns you will see the tail end of the multicolored light particles leaving your skull. Like the tail of a comet; LORD (God in you) has passed through you activating your pineal gland.

Exodus Chapter 34:2-3
> *(The LORD said)...And be ready in the morning, and come up in the morning unto the mount Si'-nai, and present thyself to me in the top of the mount. And no man shall come up with thee, neither let any man be seen throughout all the mount; neither let the flocks nor herds feed before the mount.*

"Be ready in the morning" always refers to meditation. When you are ready to meditate on the spiritual glands located in the skull (the mount), do not bring 'Animal' or 'Human' consciousness with you; still your mind so that negative and incessant thoughts have vanished.

Exodus Chapter 34:26
> *The first of the firstfruits of thy land thou shalt bring*

> *unto the house of the LORD thy God. Thou shalt not seethe a kid in his mother's milk.*

This passage is often repeated in the Bible whenever the description of opening your pineal gland is mentioned. The message here is not to return to your negative incessant thoughts. Once your spiritual centers are engaged put effort into maintaining a quieted mind. Work to stay in 'Spiritual' consciousness. Avoid regressing back to lower consciousness. This in not automatic like many people believe. People think that once you are enlightened you stay that way. No, you must continue to work at it! Yes, you are now much more capable of maintaining peace of mind but "the flesh is weak." Stay proactive in your daily encounters to stay *present*.

> Exodus Chapter 34:28
> *And he was there with the LORD forty days and forty nights; he did neither eat bread nor water.*

The number forty symbolizes the journey from lower consciousness to 'Spiritual' consciousness. Here the passage is telling us Moses' journey is complete. He has made it to 'Spiritual' consciousness. It does not literally mean that Moses stayed in his meditation for forty days and nights. In this meditation your body will be filled with divine energy. You will most likely be unable to eat or drink during this meditation—which may take several days or a week to complete.

> Exodus Chapter 34:29-30/35
> *And it came to pass, when Mo'-ses came down from the mount Si'-nai with the two tables of testimony in*

> *Mo'-ses hand, when he came down from the mount, that Mo'-ses wist not that the skin of his face shone while he talked with him. And when Aa'-ron and the children of Is'-ra-el saw Mo'-ses, behold, the skin of his face shone; and they were afraid to come nigh him... And the children of Is'-ra-el saw the face of Mo'-ses, that the skin of Mo'-ses' face shone:*

Moses' face shone. The entire resurrection (ascension) process is *energetic*. We are raising, amplifying, and purifying the energy in our bodies. After opening the pineal gland, the human body becomes full of divine energy. Moses is shining because he has literally become a light body. This is the meaning of Jesus' saying "If therefore thine eye be single, thy whole body shall be full of light." Matthew 6:22.

The rest of Exodus goes into more details on the different aspects of the spiritual center's meditation. We learn a few more significant details in the following passages:

Exodus Chapter 36:6-7
> *And Mo'-ses gave commandment, and they caused it to be proclaimed throughout the camp, saying, Let neither man nor woman make any more work for the offering of the sanctuary. So the people were restrained from bringing. For the stuff they had was sufficient for all the work to make it, and too much.*

The "work" in this meditation is your very intense breathing. During the pineal gland meditation you must breath heavily, and for an extended period of time, to generate the speed/heat necessary for Kundalini energy to pierce and activate the pineal gland. There comes a point where your breathing causes too much force. The energy becomes too fast and too hot causing your brain to go numb. You will not be able to locate or feel the pineal gland. The process is dangerously out of control. At this point your body may try to self-correct by cooling itself. This cooling is beneficial because it slows the energy down significantly so that it becomes easier to locate and strike the pineal gland with Kundalini.

Exodus Chapter 40:32-38
> *When they went into the tent of the congregation, and when they came near unto the altar, they washed; as the LORD commanded Mo'-ses. And he reared up the court round about the tabernacle and the altar, and set up hanging the gate. So Mo'-ses finished the work. Then a cloud covered the tent of the congregation, and the glory of the LORD filled the tabernacle. And Mo'-ses was not able to enter into the tent of the congregation, because the cloud abode theron, and the glory of the LORD filled the tabernacle. And when the cloud was taken up from the tabernacle, the children of Is'-ra-el went onward in all their journeys: But if the cloud were not taken up, then they journeyed not till the day that is was taken up. For the cloud of the LORD was upon the tabernacle by day, and fire was on it by night, in the sight of the house of Is-ra-el, throughout all their journeys.*

The Bible is full of cloud references for good reason. When you open your pineal gland you will have visions of clouds in your mind's eye. And you will also experience the physical presence of clouds in your meditation space. If the cloud does not appear you have not completed the pineal gland meditation.

The above passage ends Exodus. In Part Two of *Tempest in the Cloud* we will move on to the Bible's third book Leviticus. Which begins with another description of the meditation to open the pineal gland, and then moves on to the rules that people are to live by once their pineal gland is open. Yes, Leviticus is only for those who have opened their pineal glands. Once you open your pineal gland you are energetically a different person and there are special considerations for keeping yourself healthy; like not eating pork (if you haven't opened your pineal gland eat bacon without guilt!).

After Leviticus we will explore the New Testament to illustrate the ways in which the writers of those scriptures continued the same train of thought as the author's of the Old Testament. The stories in the New Testament (except those written by Paul) continue to teach the pathway to resurrection that is available to us all, as illustrated in the life of Jesus. We will unpack the meaning of why Jesus was wearing a "purple robe"[51] before he went forth into "the place of a skull"[52] as he was crucified (theorized at the age of 33) on the eve of Passover.[53] Did Jesus really die after becoming the Enlightened Christ? We will see what the esoteric version of the biblical stories in the New Testament really say about Jesus' death.

FOOTNOTES

1 Paramahansa Yogananada, The Second Coming of Christ, Self-Realization Fellowship 2004, xxi^

2 Elaine Pagels, *Revelations—Visions, Prophecy, & Politics in the Book of Revelation*, Penguin Group, New York, New York, 2012, 136—See discussion on the Catholic Church's access to Rome's political, legal, and natural resources. ^

3 Ibid., 87^

4 Ibid., 86^

5 Ibid., 162^

6 Brakke, *Athanasius and Asceticism*, 115^

7 Elaine Pagels, *Revelations—Visions, Prophecy, & Politics in the Book of Revelation*, Penguin Group, New York, New York, 2012, 157-158^

8 Ibid., 86^

9 The Secret Revelation of John, NHC I, 1, 6.19-20, In CGL vol.1, 36-37. ^

10 Elaine Pagels, *Revelations—Visions, Prophecy, & Politics in the Book of Revelation*, Penguin Group, New York, New York, 2012, 86^

11 The Secret Revelation of James, NHC II, 26.6-7, In CGL vol.2, 151. ^

12 Elaine Pagels, *Revelations—Visions, Prophecy, & Politics in the Book of Revelation*, Penguin Group, New York, New York, 2012, 100^13

Ibid., 151^

14 The Gospel of Philip 67:25-26, NHC II, 3, In CGL vol.2, 176-177. ^

15 Elaine Pagels, *Revelations—Visions, Prophecy, & Politics in the Book of Revelation*, Penguin Group, New York, New York, 2012, 152^

16 Treatise on the Resurrection, NHL I, 4, In CGL vol.1, 154-155; 48, lines 32-36, 50-151 ^

17 Elaine Pagels, *Revelations—Visions, Prophecy, & Politics in the Book of Revelation*, Penguin Group, New York, New York, 2012, 159^

18 Ibid., 156^

19 Paramahansa Yogananada, The Second Coming of Christ, Self-Realization Fellowship 2004, 69^

20 The *Mahabharata*, Vana Parva (312.117)^

21 Paramahansa Yogananada, The Second Coming of Christ, Self-Realization Fellowship 2004, 123^

22 Paramahansa Yogananada, The Second Coming of Christ, Self-Realization Fellowship 2004, 46^

23 Paramahansa Yogananada, The Second Coming of Christ, Self-Realization Fellowship 2004, 93^

24 Paramahansa Yogananada, The Second Coming of Christ, Self-Realization Fellowship 2004, 22^

25 Swami Satyananda Saraswati, *Kundalini Tantra*. Bihar School of Yoga, 1984, 23^

26 Swami Satyananda Saraswati, *Kundalini Tantra*. Bihar School of Yoga, 1984, 25^

27 Swami Satyananda Saraswati, *Kundalini Tantra*. Bihar School of Yoga, 1984, 25^

28 Swami Satyananda Saraswati, *Kundalini Tantra*. Bihar School of Yoga, 1984, 25^

29 Swami Satyananda Saraswati, *Kundalini Tantra*. Bihar School of Yoga, 1984, 123^

30 Swami Satyananda Saraswati, *Kundalini Tantra*. Bihar School of Yoga, 1984, 36^

31 Paramahansa Yogananada, The Second Coming of Christ, Self-Realization Fellowship 2004, 121^32

 The Holy Bible King James Version, 3:1^

33 Paramahansa Yogananada, The Second Coming of Christ, Self-Realization Fellowship 2004, 144^

34 The Holy Bible King James Version Genesis 3:23^

35 Mysteriously there is no record of Jesus' exact age at the time of his death. But many references place his death at or near 33. Luke 3:23 states Jesus started his ministry at around the age of 30. Paramahansa Yogananada states in his book *The Second Coming of Christ* that Jesus' ministry lasted

"three years." ^

36 Paramahansa Yogananada, The Second Coming of Christ, Self-Realization Fellowship 2004, 60^

37 The Holy Bible King James Version Genesis 9:15^

38 Ibid., Exodus 25:6^

39 Ibid., Genesis 32:30^

40 Paramahansa Yogananada, The Second Coming of Christ, Self-Realization Fellowship 2004, 109^

41 Paramahansa Yogananada, The Second Coming of Christ, Self-Realization Fellowship 2004, xxv^

42 Paramahansa Yogananada, The Second Coming of Christ, Self-Realization Fellowship 2004, 113^

43 Paramahansa Yogananada, The Second Coming of Christ, Self-Realization Fellowship 2004, 20^

44 Paramahansa Yogananada, The Second Coming of Christ, Self-Realization Fellowship 2004, 1378^

45 Rambam on Maaser Sheni 2:4^

46 Strong's #7827^

47 Swami Satyananda Saraswati, *Kundalini Tantra*. Bihar School of Yoga, 1984, 192^

48 Swami Satyananda Saraswati, *Kundalini Tantra*. Bihar School of Yoga, 1984, 124^

49 Paramahansa Yogananada, The Second Coming of Christ, Self-Realization Fellowship 2004, 110^

50 Paramahansa Yogananada, The Second Coming of Chr ist, Self-Realization Fellowship 2004, 32^

51 The Holy Bible King James Version John 19:5^

52 Ibid., John 19:17^

53 Ibid., John 19:14

www.ingramcontent.com/pod-product-compliance
Lightning Source LLC
Chambersburg PA
CBHW062112290426
44110CB00023B/2787